LUBENHAM

A village history

Lubenham Heritage Group

Copyright © 2012 Lubenham Heritage Group

All rights reserved. No part of this publication may be reproduced, distributed, or transmitted in any form or by any means, including photocopying, recording, or other electronic or mechanical methods, without the prior written permission of the publisher.

ISBN: 978-0-9573815-0-6

Published by
Lubenham Heritage Group
137 Main Street
Lubenham
Leicestershire LE16 9TG

Printed by Cambrian Printers
Aberystwyth

Contents

		Page
Acknowledgements		iii
Maps		iv
Introduction		1
1.	In the Past	3
2.	Getting around – road, rail and canal	13
3.	Church and Chapel	25
4.	School days – education and learning	33
5.	Mansions and cottages	41
6.	Earning a living	57
7.	Village characters	73
8.	War and remembrance	79
9.	Time off – leisure and recreation	85
10.	Horses and hunting	101
11.	Tales of Papillon Hall	107
	Appendix: Lubenham in the early 1900's	110
	List of illustrations	115
	Index	117

Acknowledgements

Following the success of the Lubenham Heritage Trail launched in 2009 it was suggested that our committee should write a book about the history and heritage of the village. However, this would not have been possible without the help of members of the Heritage Group and the people of Lubenham who have generously given time and support to the project. We are grateful to all of you.

We should like to thank especially Leicestershire County Council, Harborough Museum, Leicestershire & Rutland Records Office and the *Leicester Mercury* for allowing us to reproduce material; Lubenham Parish Council, Lubenham Scarecrow Committee, Café Onyx and other local groups and individuals who have given funds towards the production of this book; professional photographers Andrew Carpenter and Jonathan Clark as well as all those members of the community who have so generously donated photographs and other information; artists Elizabeth Wells, June Moore, Rosemary Slough, Eileen & Roger Wild and members of Lubenham Art Group. Names included in the List of Illustrations are some indication of the number of people to whom we are indebted. Our sincere apologies if we have inadvertently omitted anyone, but we certainly have not forgotten your contribution. We have made every effort to trace and credit copyright owners.

Thanks are also due to John Dyke and Annette Deacon for going through the script and altering our numerous mistakes. Any errors in the book are entirely our responsibility.

However our most sincere thanks must go to Geoff Ellis who volunteered (rashly in our opinion!) to plan and design the layout of the book. He gave up many hours of his time, completely free of charge, and without his help and advice, this project would not have been possible.

Barbara Burbidge, David Carter, Pat Dyke & David Hannibal
Lubenham Heritage Group

Left: Lubenham got its moment of Olympic glory in 2012 when the torch came through the village on its nationwide tour. It was carried by charity fundraiser Rob Gomez, the chairman of Bowden Cricket Club.

Maps

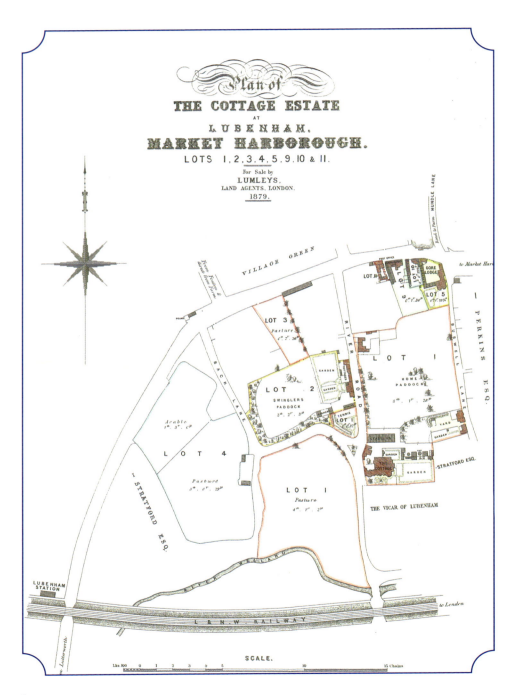

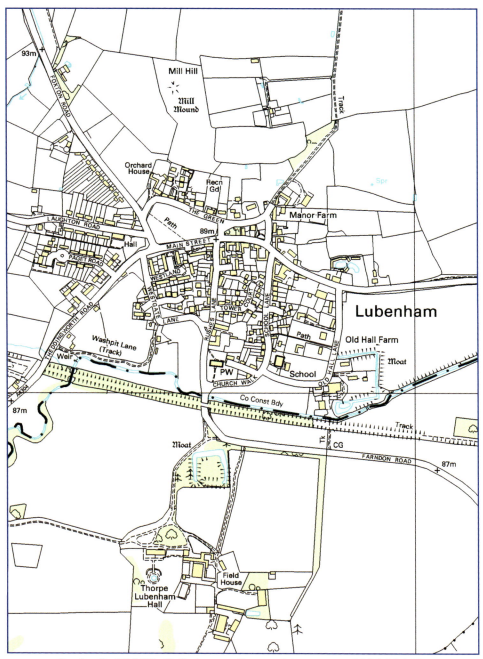

Scale: 1: 10000. © Ordnance Survey. Licence no 100040443.

Left: Lubenham in 1879 when the Cottage Estate came up for sale.
Not only was the village a lot smaller than it is today **(see above)**
but many of the street names were also different.

v

Introduction

Introduction

Nestling in the lee of Mill Hill, Lubenham lies two miles west of Market Harborough in the valley of the River Welland. A quintessential English village, it is a compact, nucleated settlement of around 1000 people which, even with the main road and the proximity of a large market town, has managed to retain its rural identity and community spirit.

'*Lubenham is very much a community alive, enthusiastic and responsive*' was a comment made by the judges who voted it the Central England regional winner in the prestigious Calor Village of the Year awards. It is a statement which embodies the ethos and character of the village.

The origins of this book begin in 2009 when the Heritage Group launched the Lubenham Heritage Trail. Comprising a leaflet, central information board and plaques on selected buildings, it was designed to encourage residents and visitors alike to find out more about this attractive and yet often under-rated village. Such was its success that many suggested that the Heritage Group should write a book. This seemed like a good idea as we could draw on previous research and had already collected a large quantity of information for both the leaflet and presentations given at Heritage Group meetings but, as is often the case, things were not that straightforward!

One of the most difficult decisions was what and how much to include as we did not want the end result to be either superficial or too detailed and academic. In the end, we decided against a chronological approach, preferring instead to look at the history and development of the village through the lives of ordinary people and the institutions, customs and traditions which affected them such as the church, the school, employment and leisure.

Numerous other commitments meant that the planned publication date was put back several times. Finally, we grasped the nettle and decided, come what may, that we would publish in the Queen's Diamond Jubilee year, 2012.

We hope the book is both informative and enjoyable and provides a view of life in our village.

The Lubenham Heritage Group
July 2012

Lubenham Heritage Group

Lubenham Heritage Group was formed in 2001 after it was recognised that many people were interested in the history and heritage of the village. It is a lively and thriving group which takes an active role in the life and affairs of the community.

We hold monthly meetings of lectures and talks, many involving local people on topics specific to Lubenham, as well as organising special events for our members.

The Group has produced the Lubenham Heritage Trail, comprising a highly successful leaflet, central information board and plaques on notable buildings, and published the Lubenham Parish Walks leaflet in conjunction with Leicester-shire County Council.

Enquiries about the village are received from many parts of the country and abroad. New members and friends are always welcome.

In the Past

From the Domesday Book compiled for William the Conqueror

1. In the Past

In common with many places in England, the origins of the village of Lubenham are lost in the mists of time. The discovery of a rare hand axe just across the river at Marston Trussell proves human activity in the area dating back to the Middle Palaeolithic. Archaeological work associated with the development of the Airfield Farm site in the parish has recorded the presence of a trackway, two adjoining enclosures and a central roundhouse used for domestic purposes, together with sherds of pottery dating from the Middle to Late Iron Age (400BC to 42AD).

It is generally believed that Lubenham developed near a shallow but important crossing of the River Welland. Even today with modern technology this small, innocuous river is liable to flood and it is highly probable that in the past, especially during the winter months, the valley would have been wet and almost impassable. The Undle (sometimes called Hundle, probably meaning 'under the hill') is widely believed to be an ancient trackway, leading from the river and beyond to the higher, fertile ground north of the village. The recently discovered Iron Age settlement along this route adds weight to the theory. Little is known about an east–west route although it is likely that a trackway along the river valley, probably above the flood plain, would have linked the area to the east and the important Bronze Age route which followed the higher ground from Welford through Husbands Bosworth to Tilton on the Hill.

Roman occupation in Lubenham is much less clear. Both Nichols[1] and the *History of the County of Leicestershire*[2] record what was believed to be a Roman camp in a field to the east of Lubenham but this theory is now dismissed as the remains are almost certainly mediaeval. Despite lack of firm evidence, Roman activity in Lubenham itself cannot be discounted. Archaeological work in the parish on the

Airfield Farm site in 2010/11 recorded a series of enclosures and sherds of pottery dating from this period[3] and there are known Roman remains scattered throughout the area including finds of pottery in nearby Marston Trussell and evidence of a Roman camp at East Farndon.

The name Lubenham is widely believed to have come from the Saxon 'Lubba's ham' or 'the homestead of Lubba'. The suffix 'ham' does indeed suggest Saxon origins but as early recorded spellings include Lobenho, Lubnam, Lubanha and Lodenham, there is still debate as to the actual derivation of the name. It is now understood that the original Anglo Saxon settlements in this area were small farmsteads occupied by extended families which were later, probably in 8th and 9th centuries, replaced by villages and small towns. Little is known about Anglo Saxon Lubenham as most buildings were constructed of wood and evidence, other than some sherds of pottery unearthed during field walking, has long since disappeared. However, village life and development would have been influenced by the many changes taking place in the country.

Leicestershire was part of the Saxon kingdom of Mercia until large parts of Eastern and Central England were ceded to the Danes in 878AD. The Danelaw, as it was known, lasted for less that 50 years but in that time the Danes stamped their authority on the language, customs and administration of the area, influences which still survive today. For administrative purposes, especially for the collection of taxes, the land was divided into areas known as Wapentakes or Hundreds. Lubenham lay in the Gartree Hundred. Sometime around 917 the area was restored to Saxon rule and by the time of Edward the Confessor (1033 to 1066AD) the land around the village, comprising eight ploughlands (a plough is the amount of land which could be ploughed in a year by a team of eight oxen), was held by Osmund, Archil and Oslac.

William of Normandy's victory at Hastings in 1066 brought radical changes in England. He eradicated Saxon power through often brutal warfare, built imposing castles and fortifications, whilst impressive cathedrals stamped Norman authority over religious life. Saxon landowners were dispossessed and replaced by William's most loyal supporters. A stringent feudal system, based on tenancy rather than

Hundred – large administrative sub-division of a county, each having its own representative body from local villages. Equivalent to a Wapentake in Danelaw counties.

Carucate – measure of land, approx. 120 acres, which a team of eight oxen could plough in a year.

Demesne – land belonging to the Lord of the Manor.

Freeman – class of peasant possessing a relatively strong economic position.

Villein – serf who has legal status of a freeman in all except his dealings with the lord.

Bordar – a villein who rendered manual service in return for his cottage.

Bondman/bondwoman – someone bound to labour without wages. A slave.

ownership, was introduced. However, much of the basic framework of rural Anglo-Saxon England survived as boundaries of estates and parishes remained virtually intact and the agricultural population was substantially unaltered.

What happened in Lubenham in the aftermath of 1066 is speculative but it is known that William's troops laid waste to farmland and decimated crops in this area and that nearby Leicester was substantially destroyed.

The Domesday Survey of 1086 details the situation in Lubenham 20 years after the Conquest when the population was recorded as 45. Every village was required to supply information on the identity of the landowners, the amount of land they held, its value at the time of the Conquest and at present (1086) and the use to which the land was put. The thoroughness of the survey was summarised in the *Anglo-Saxon Chronicle*: 'not even one ox or one cow or one pig escaped notice'.

William granted the land in Lubenham to the Archbishop of York, Countess Judith and Robert de Todini, Lord of Belvoir, fees which probably corresponded to the pre-1066 holdings of the three Saxon tenants. The precise whereabouts of these lands and the number of actual manor houses is unknown. It is likely that some of the land in Lubenham was attached to manors elsewhere.

The fee granted to Robert de Todini was valued at 10 shillings per annum at the time of Edward the Confessor and 20 shillings in 1086. He held two carucates (around 240 acres) of which 1½ carucates were with the demesne (manor). Six villeins with two bordars had one plough. There were 10 acres of meadow.

Countess Judith, the niece of William I, was granted considerable land holdings in the Midlands and Eastern England. She was married to Earl Waltheof, a prominent Saxon who had been allowed to keep his lands after swearing allegiance to William but who became involved in the Earl's Revolt of 1075 and was beheaded. Later, when Judith refused to marry Simon de Senlis, first Earl of Northampton, William confiscated her lands and she fled the country.

The fee held by Judith in Lubenham amounted to seven carucates (approximately 840 acres) which were valued annually at 50 shillings (10 shillings pre-1066). At the time of Domesday they were under the tenure of Robert de Buci as part of a larger estate in Foxton and Gumley. In the demesne there were two ploughs and three bondmen; eight villeins with three bordars and two Frenchmen had four ploughs. There were 20 acres of meadow. It is presumed that this land was given by Judith's son, Earl Simon, to Robert of Foxton and that subsequently the overlordship of the holding in Lubenham probably followed that of Foxton.

The largest fee of eight carucates (960 acres) was granted to the Archbishop of York, but was held by Walchelin who again transferred it to Robert. The annual value of 20 shillings at the time of the Confessor had risen to 40 shillings by Domesday. In the demesne were two ploughs, two bondmen and two bondwomen. Six villeins with four bordars had three ploughs. Three carucates were held by another Robert, a knight, who employed one plough in his demesne. Five villeins with one bordar had 1½ ploughs. There were 36 acres of meadow.

What is known about Lubenham from the 12th to 16th centuries is based largely on the history of the Church and Manor. It is a complicated and confusing story in which many names appear in the records.

The fee held by Osbern under Robert de Todini in 1086 is difficult to trace. It was held in the 15th and 16th century by a family called Brampton but all references disappear from the mid 16th century onwards.

In 1220 the demesne tenant on the land which had passed to Robert of Foxton (formerly the fee of Countess Judith) was John le Poer, but by 1247 he had been replaced by John and Lettice Mallesours. A descendant, Anne Mallesours, married Roger Prestwyche in the mid 14th century and the Prestwyche family remained Lords of the Manor for five generations.

The fee held by the Archbishop of York was part of the Trussell estate until 1240 when the land was divided between Peter de Wolwardington and Nicholas de Baud. Wolwardington is mentioned in the church records as they and the Bauds held the advowson alternatively but little is known about the family. The Bauds on the other hand were more prominent, the present Old Hall was formerly known as Baud's Manor.[4]

The Baud crest

William de Baud came to England at the time of the Conquest and was granted lands in Hadham, Hertfordshire where records show he built a Hall surrounded by a stockade and moat. This survived for 350 years until it was replaced in 1440 by a brick construction at about the same time the manor in Lubenham was sold. The present Hadham Hall is rather splendid but much altered in Elizabethan times. The Bauds held several other manors in Hertfordshire and Essex and it is not known if any members of the family actually lived in Lubenham, although connections with All Saints Church are recorded.

England in the 13th century was undergoing considerable change. Although the open field system[5] still dominated rural life, as it would for a further 500 years, there was growth in other crafts and trades. Markets were opening where peasants could sell their surplus and lease stalls. Free peasants, including women, were beginning to have more say over their lives, literacy was increasing and some freemen became clerks, chaplains and reeves. It was the beginning of the tax system and Court Rolls show that even the poorest that held a cottage, land or shop in the market were taxed.

What influence significant national events had on Lubenham is hard to tell. Magna Carta (1215 and modified through 13th century) was the first document forced on an English king by his subjects. It required King John to proclaim certain liberties, notably that no freeman could be punished except through the law of the land.

The Baron's War 1262–4, led by Simon de Montfort, Earl of Leicester, was provoked by Henry III's methods of government and higher tax demands which coincided with severe famine. Henry was taken prisoner at the Battle of Lewes in 1264 and de Montfort became *de facto* ruler of England with an elected Parliament until defeated and killed a year later at the Battle of Evesham. It is known that men from the Gartree Hundred fought for de Montfort at Lewes but it is not clear if this included any from Lubenham.

The 14th century was a period of great upheaval. The population was growing and there was pressure on land and resources. Wars with France and Scotland led to an increase in tax demands, but worse was to come. A succession of wet summers and frozen winters from 1315 to 1318 coinciding with a disease which killed around 60 per cent of the cattle, led to widespread famine in which the poor were disproportionately affected. An epidemic of typhoid and dysentery was to follow and it is estimated that 10 per cent of the population in England died in this period.

Lubenham would have certainly been affected by these tragic events but by 1327 the situation had improved sufficiently for William Baud to obtain permission to hold two weekly markets, on Wednesdays and Saturdays, and an annual fair at Whitsuntide at the manor. Such fairs and markets were popular. The Lord of the Manor charged rent on the stalls and peasants could sell their surplus, but their presence was often disputed by neighbouring gentry. Richard de Loterington of Thorpe Lubenham and Ralph Mallesours of Foxton were both vehemently opposed to the market. Indeed, Mallesours had to answer two charges of malicious damage to stalls and wares and assaults on officials and customers in 1330 and again in 1335. The market in Lubenham was short-lived mainly, it is thought, due to competition from nearby Harborough.

Poll tax records show that life in the country was prospering until the Black Death arrived in the summer of 1348. By the end of the following year the plague had spread across the whole country, killing around a third of the population. The number who died in Lubenham is not known but Michael Wood's graphic account of what happened in nearby Kibworth may be an indication.[6]

After the Black Death there were not enough workers nationally to work the land and the economy had to adapt to meet the changing social conditions. Land was put down to pasture, boosting the number of sheep and the woollen industry; landlords were forced to lease their land and peasants became more mobile, responding to the greater demand for their labour and higher wages. However, the basic feudal structure still remained and the economic prosperity was short-lived.

In 1421 the descendants of the Wolwardington family sold their land to William Tresham and the following year Thomas Palmer acquired Baud's Manor from Thomas and Margery Baud together with eight messuages (a dwelling with outhouses and adjacent land), two tofts (a homestead), one watermill, nine virgates of land (approximately 30 acres), 40 acres of pasture and rent amounting to 2s 1d. The actual site of the watermill is unknown. First mentioned in 13th century, it may have been on that stretch of the river between the Church and east of the Old Hall which was straightened during the building of the railway in 1849. Also there is a field near the Marston Trussell road known as Burnt Mill which has interesting features.

According to the Feet of Fines (a legal way of conveying property) dated 8th July 1442 Thomas Baud granted Thomas Palmer 'the rent, together with homages and all services of John Smyth, Richard Perewych, John Taillour, William Taillour, Joan Mouseley, John Brook, Walter Colyn and William Lord and their heirs, in respect of all the tenements which they held before of Thomas Baud in the aforesaid vill.'

> **Feet of Fines:** Three copies were made on a single sheet of parchment and then separated by cutting along indented (wavy) lines to prevent forgery.
> The copy from the foot of the page was retained by the Court, hence the Feet of Fines, or final agreement.

Palmer was succeeded by his son-in-law William Nevill. In 1478 Palmer's widow Elizabeth and her heirs gave up the right to the advowson of the church in Lubenham to William Chauntry, Dean of Leicester.

It appears that in a Feet of Fines dated 3rd February 1500, the manor and tenements passed to Richard and Eleanor Perewych and their heirs 'to hold of the chief lords'. The property was listed as the Manor of Lubenham and 20 messuages, 300 acres of land, 100 acres of meadow, 200 acres of pasture, 20 acres of wood and 20 shillings of rent.

In 1553 Henry Brooke made an agreement with his stepson William Digby, a descendant of the Prestwyche family, to acquire the manor. He was succeeded by his cousin Roger and nephew Andrew and in 1569 by Andrew's son Sir Basil Brooke.

In 1563 there were 60 families living in the village, most of whom would be employed in agriculture, working the open field system. However, Lubenham was soon to be hit by the plague. In 1583, 24 deaths were recorded and entries in the Parish Church Records read *'Jan 18 1583 sicknes begininge'*, *'March 22 1583 sicknes still'*, *'June 18 1583 sicknes ceased. God be praysed'*. The plague returned and from 30th July 1604 to 10th April 1605, 83 deaths were recorded, including Margery Smith and four children and Robert Cartar, his wife and three children.

In 1600 Basil Brook was in financial difficulty, claiming his income from the Manor House and annual rent of £300 from 13 farms was insufficient.[7] He made an agreement to enclose some land with 17 independent freeholders who received a proportion of 16 acres for every 15 acres of their former holdings. As a result 120 acres of arable were converted to pasture as well as 51 acres belonging to tenants and three small farms were broken up. Brooke still retained 10 arable farms and when his son sold the Manor to Randolph Crewe 24 years later the property included 10 messuages, six cottages and a windmill which stood on Mill Hill until destroyed by fire in 1886/7.

Conversion from arable to pasture meant unemployment as fewer men were needed to work the land. Early enclosures resulted in a large number of freeholders with small estates in the village, the consequences of which can still be seen today in the number of medium sized houses dating from the 17th century.[8] In 1630 some of the freeholders were named as Job Boyce, Edward Cotton, William Spriggs, Robert Croft, William Hartshorne, Oliver Sprigg, Robert Welford and Henry Neale.

The Crewe family who held the Manor from 1624 to 1733 were absentee landlords. The manor house was leased to local farmers including a Mr Collins, who was tenant when Charles I stayed at the Old Hall before the Battle of Naseby in 1645.

By 1722 there were 23 freeholders in the parish. Eleven years later, the manor, several farms and premises with an annual value of £700 and described at the sale as 'capable of great improvements' were sold to Samuel Wright. He com-

Mill Hill windmill

The iron pole-end still remains on site, indicating the mill had a wooden windshaft and that the sails were of spring or canvas type as there is no striking rod hole.

Nigel Moon, *Windmills of Leicestershire and Rutland.* Sycamore, 1981

In the Past

> ### The Battle of Naseby
>
> On June 14th 1645 the Parliamentarian New Model Army led by Oliver Cromwell inflicted a heavy defeat on the Royalist forces of Charles I at the Battle of Naseby.
>
> The Royalists, moving south from Leicester, reached Market Harborough on the 13th. Charles, staying at the Old Hall in Lubenham, was woken from his sleep to be told that the opposing forces were encamped around Guilsborough, only a few miles to the south, and that some skirmishes had already taken place.
>
> The two armies met the following day in fields near the village of Naseby. It was the decisive battle of the Civil War. Although the conflict dragged on for another year, the Royalists never recovered from the severe losses they had sustained and Charles finally surrendered in May 1646.

missioned a survey of the lands, a description of which can be found in Chapter 6, *Earning a Living*.

Wright died in 1735 and left the manor to a distant cousin and his family. Around 1800 John Wright moved from the dilapidated Old Hall[8] to a fine Queen Anne house on the Green, now known as Manor Farm, taking the Lordship of the Manor with him. The farm was mortgaged in 1827 to Richard Mitchell who was later ruined by the failure of a Leicester bank and the property and Lordship were purchased by Thomas Paget of Humberstone. Paget and his heirs, Thomas Tertius, Guy and Reginald, never lived at Manor Farm. The land and house were eventually sold in 1980s–90s and the title Lord of the Manor purchased by the owner of the Old Hall, so restoring it to its historic home.

The parish was finally enclosed by the Enclosure Act of 1766 and Chapter 6 describes the effect this had on the village. Conditions for the poor were particularly harsh; there was high unemployment among weavers and in agriculture. Between 1784 and 1792, 54 people in the village were buried as paupers.

During the 18th century the parish was administered by two Churchwardens, two Overseers of the Poor, two Surveyors of Highways and a Constable, all elected annually at the Easter Vestry, a meeting which administered the affairs of the parish. Parish records giving detailed and graphic accounts of life in the village are housed at the Leicestershire Records Office. The documents include accounts of the Churchwardens (1712–1941), Constables (1744–1828), Overseers of the Poor (1761–1835) and Overseers of the Highways (1710–1852).

The position of the poor in Lubenham is of particular interest. Overseers were established in England in 1601 with the power to collect a local tax to help the poor who could not work, such as the old or disabled, and to provide work for the able-bodied. The Overseers were unpaid and often churchwardens or local landowners were selected. Goods belonging to the poor became the property of the parish and in return paupers were housed, clothed and looked after. There are many examples in the Lubenham records of inventories such as the following from the 1760s:

– *Widow Palmer's goods: one bed and bedding, two wheels and one reel, two tables, three chairs, three boxes, one oven pot, a pair of bellows and pot hooks.*
– *Mary Smalley's goods: bed and bedding, one box, reel and wheel, one chair and one bell metal pot.*
– *Peter Luck's goods: a bed and bedding, dough trough, table and iron pot.*

In 1723 a law was passed allowing parishes to build workhouses with the first known reference to one in Lubenham dating from 1762/3, believed to be on Westgate Lane. Nine years later William Ashby was paid £45 for a property on the same lane which was to be converted into a new workhouse. By 1802/3 there were 70 adults and 116 children receiving outdoor relief and only 10 people in the workhouse.

It was common practice for paupers from elsewhere who did not have a permit to be sent back to their own village so that they did not become the responsibility of the incoming parish. One unusual case was that of Robert Tilley who, although born in Lubenham, was ordered by the Justices of the Peace to be returned to Hallaton with his wife as they 'have come to inhabit in the said parish of Lubenham not having gained a legal settlement there nor producing a certificate owning them to be settled elsewhere and that the said Robert Tilley and Ann his wife are likely to be chargeable to the said parish of Lubenham.'[9] However, they came back to Lubenham four days later and their descendants still live in the village.

Help was given to paupers who wanted to emigrate to America, part of the cost being met by the Poor Rate. A Vestry meeting of 1833 agreed that Henry Gilbert, George Cockerill, Will Sprigg, George Ashton, Richard Swingler, Will Goode and B. Riddington 'shall have their expenses paid over the water and £4 when they arrive in America'. It was normal to travel by canal boat to Liverpool where they boarded a ship.

In 1824 the Overseers of the Poor purchased three houses for £90 from a Mr Glover of Kilby and sometime later nine houses known as Coleman's Row from Mr Coleman of Lubenham for

> ### Proceedings of the Old Bailey
> (ref: t17660116–3) 16th January 1766
>
> ## JOSEPH WILFORD, THEFT: ANIMAL THEFT
>
> According to the original text of the court proceedings, Joseph Wilford of Lubenham was indicted for stealing a bay gelding belonging to John Wright (Lord of the Manor) on December 31st 1765.
>
> The keeper and ostler of *The Sun* in Gray's Inn Lane, London, both stated that Wilford had tried to sell the horse, which they recognised as stolen from an entry in *The Advertiser*, for $7^1/_2$ guineas. In his defence, Wilford claimed he had bought the animal from a man near Oakham.
>
> Despite the testimony of several character witnesses, Wilford was found guilty with a recommendation for the death penalty, but there is evidence that he was actually transported to America on the convict ship *Justitia* in September 1766. He married, settled in Pennsylvania and became a Justice of the Peace.

£200. The situation changed in 1834 when Parliament passed the Poor Law Act. This deemed that no able-bodied person was to receive money or aid from the authorities except in a workhouse, where conditions were deliberately harsh, to discourage people from wanting help. Workhouses were to be built in every parish or, where too small, a union of parishes, and there had to be a Board of Governors. Overseers were now paid a wage and in that year Thomas Eldridge of Lubenham received an annual salary of £20. In 1836 the parish was included in the Market Harborough Union.

In 1864 the Privy Council commissioned Dr Julian Hunter to look into the housing accommodation for agricultural and other labourers in rural districts. He examined 5,375 different dwellings in various counties and enquired into the local circumstances of each district. Poverty and poor living conditions were well known in urban areas but Dr Hunter's report, published in 1865, makes equally depressing reading. Lubenham was one of the parishes singled out and, as an article in *The Spectator* on 22nd April 1865 describes, 'everywhere Dr Hunter found the same evils – some villages in which the crowding has destroyed all comfort, all sense of physical decency, and not infrequently all morality ... one case (Lubenham) must be given as a feeble hint of the true state of affairs'.

Of the 35 houses selected in the village, 22 had only one bedroom. Poverty forced the largest families into the smallest houses. In one bedroom lived a married couple, two boys of 20 and 18, a girl of 17 and a grandchild. In another there was a married couple with five children. Other examples from the village include a married pair and two adult sons; four adults and two children; a widower, his two sons, two daughters and their two children; six adults and two children, although in this case there was a lean-to outbuilding in which some slept.

Local newspapers of the time record several tragic events in the village, especially during the 1890s. There were at least four suicides or attempted suicides between 1890 and 1895: Walter Goode, a farm labourer aged 16; Edwin Cowby aged 17; John Pickering a gardener aged 55; and Charles Ashton. An elderly woman, Eliza Osborne (72), lost her life in a fire in August 1899. Five years earlier a four-year-old child, Ada Brookes, the daughter of an engine driver, died from the effects of poisoning. The inquest held at the *Paget Arms* concluded that she had eaten some poisonous berries, thought to be yew, which grew in the school grounds. Her six-year-old sister survived.

Perhaps the most distressing case is that of the death of the 12-month-old daughter of Joshua Perkins. A report on the inquest, held in the *Red Cow* on 19th November 1845, appeared in the *Northampton Mercury* the following Saturday:

> *From the evidence before the coroner it appeared that Mrs Perkins and the servant girl were washing on Monday last, when the child was placed in a high chair against the table. The servant took a pan full of boiling water and poured upon some clothes in a panshon standing near the child, and left the room for the purpose of refilling the pan, when the child, by leaning too far over the arm of the chair, overbalanced and fell into the scalding water. The head and upper part of the body were severely injured and on Tuesday morning the little sufferer expired.*
> *Verdict – accidental death.*

However, many changes were taking place at this time and are described elsewhere in this book. These included transport, especially the coming of the railway; the shift in emphasis from agriculture to other employment, most notably Victoria Mills; and the establishment of the village school.

The population increased from 504 at the turn of the century to 683 in 1891 and there were improvements to the standards of living. There were numerous wells in and around Lubenham, but in 1856 the Select Vestry applied to the Poor Law Board for permission to pay for an improved water supply from parochial funded properties. It was not successful but three years later it established a sewer authority under the provision of the Sanitary Act which immediately set about cleaning the parish pond, erecting a new pump and laying drains.

The first mention of a piped water supply in the village was in the minutes of the Local Board in 1891 when Mr Harter of Lubenham Hall was charged £31 p.a. for water supply. Minutes from May 1893 show water was to be supplied to the Inn at Lubenham for £5 p.a. and to an unspecified house at £10 p.a.

Local administration was also changing. There was a need to rationalise the piecemeal development that had taken place over the centuries and in 1888 the Local Government Act created administrative counties based on the historic boundaries. Another Act, in 1894, created a second tier of local government whereby counties were divided into rural or urban districts, and Parish Councils were established. Lubenham Parish Council started in 1894 with six councillors, the number still current in 2012.

The population of the parish has doubled in the 20th century from 618 in 1901 to 1285 in 2001, with a marked increase since the 1930s. The physical expansion and growth in the number of houses, changes in agriculture and employment, the demise of the railway, local shops and services are described elsewhere in this book. In the 21st century Lubenham is becoming a commuter village where people live but work elsewhere. However, unlike many other villages it has maintained a staunch community spirit and a sense of belonging.

References

[1] Nichols, John. *The History and Antiquities of the County of Leicester*, volume II, part II, 1798.

[2] *History of the County of Leicestershire*. Volume 5: Gartree Hundred, 1964.

[3] Clarke, J. *Archaeological evaluation of land at Airfield Farm, Market Harborough*. Unpublished manuscript, 2010.

[4] See Chapter 5, *Mansions and cottages*.

[5] See Chapter 6, *Earning a living*.

[6] Wood, Michael. *The Story of England*. Viking, 2010.

[7] See Chapter 6, *Earning a living*.

[8] See Chapter 5, *Mansions and cottages*.

[9] *Overseers of the Poor Report*, November 1778.

Getting Around

2. Getting around – road, rail and canal

Roads past and present

Little is known about the earliest tracks but it is likely that some of these ancient routes are still in use today as footpaths and bridleways, linking Lubenham to neighbouring communities or leading to important places in the village such as the river.

The trackway through the village from a shallow crossing of the River Welland, along Undle Lane to the higher ground beyond, is thought to date from the Iron Age, a belief strengthened by recent archaeological work which has revealed nearby evidence of two enclosures, one with a central roundhouse. There is little sign of Roman roads in the immediate area but the important Gartree Road lies only a few miles to the north.

Leicester was an important centre in the Anglo Saxon and Danish periods. At the same time, several settlements were developing on the wide open lands in the south of the county, with evidence of Saxon pottery recently unearthed in Lubenham parish itself. It is reasonable to presume that a network of roads and tracks evolved to link these various settlements and that the pattern of main roads had begun to take shape well before the Conquest.

During the Middle Ages the growth of trade and the establishment of towns meant that an improved road system was needed. Two main routes crossed this part of the county linking the influential mediaeval towns of Northampton and Leicester; one an ancient track followed a ridge of high land through nearby Husbands Bosworth and Welford and another which passed through Harborough. Although not shown on the earliest maps, it is almost certain that a route taking important east–west traffic was in existence and probably passed through Lubenham. At this time road repair was undertaken by the Lord of the Manor but this gradually changed and by Tudor times highway maintenance became the responsibility of the parish. Parishioners with teams of horses and carts were pressed into service to work four days a year after harvest under a Surveyor of Highways.[1]

The Undle, believed to be an ancient trackway running up to the fertile higher ground north of the village.

The introduction of the Turnpike system led to the transformation of road maintenance, although improvements did not happen overnight. The same methods of repair were used until John McAdam (1757–1834) introduced his more efficient and relatively cheap method of road building. The first Act allowing the erection of gates and charging of tolls on a stretch of The Great North Road was passed in 1663. The Turnpike system reached this area some 58 years later when two roads from Northampton, one via Welford Bridge, the other at the Chain Bridge in Market Harborough, came under the Act. It was not until 1754–5, in the reign of George II, that the road from Harborough to Coventry through Lubenham became a turnpike. Unfortunately, the precise location of the original six toll gates is not known and there are no surviving records of the tolls charged or amount collected annually. Several Continuation Acts, which extended the operation for a further term, were passed during the reigns of George III and IV until the end came with the Expiry Act on 31st December 1874. The turnpike road in Lubenham had lasted 120 years.

Late 19th century cast iron milepost situated on Main Street near the junction with Paget Road

Robberies along this stretch of the road were not unknown. The *Leicester Chronicle* of October 9th 1841 reported that a travelling draper was stopped between Lubenham and Harborough by three men armed with cudgels. Unfortunately for the robbers their victim had previously worked on board ship and knew how to defend himself. As the newspaper comments, 'the scamps will be cautious how they again stop a travelling draper'!

Mr Benjamin Giddington was not so fortunate. In December 1858 he was returning home when he was stopped by three men who put a plaster over his face and robbed him of £4.12.6d, around £360 in today's terms.

In 1888 Parliament set up County Councils. These took over the maintenance of the principal routes, often the former turnpikes, whilst the secondary roads became the responsibility of Urban or Rural District Councils. The main road through Lubenham eventually became the A427, now A4304. Other roads, most notably to Foxton, Laughton and East Farndon, were little more than gated field roads until World War II.

As to be expected, the earliest cars in the village were found at the larger houses including Thorpe Lubenham Hall, Papillon Hall and The Hill, where a separate chauffeur's cottage was built in 1924. The Hollies on Main Street, one of the properties owned by the Perkins family, boasted a garage complete with inspection pit.

The Coach and Horses – a coaching inn

Formerly *The White Swan*, a date stone 1700 SJA suggests it pre-dates the Turnpike era. An 1879 sales catalogue lists facilities typical of a coaching inn – stables, loose box, blacksmith's shop, forge, carriage yard and small paddock.

A beam behind the bar reads 'Happy the house the goods whereof excel when the owners godly and those gotton well. WS HC 1610'.

> Serious trap accident near Lubenham Station at 6pm on Tuesday evening. Two vehicles, one driven by Mr Ricketts, bailiff of Sulby Lodge, and the other by Mr Measham, coachman to Mr Soames of Papillon Hall, collided.
>
> *Northampton Mercury, 31st October 1902*

Through traffic, especially lorries, used the main road and as the number of vehicles increased, garages opened in the village. In 1946 permission was granted for a petrol pump in Rushes Lane, with the facilities extended six years later. It remained open until 1985. In 1947 another garage opened on Main Street which was gradually enlarged to include a workshop, car sales room and later a small shop and village post office. This garage closed in 2006.

Above: Main Street in 1910 before the advent of mass motoring.
Below: Maddever's garage in Rushes Lane, which closed in 1985.

Getting Around

Badgers Garage on Main Street, a petrol station, garage, car sales centre and (in its last couple of years) a small shop-cum-newsagent. **Above:** awaiting demolition in 2006 to make way for housing. **Below:** It is now the site of The Hawthorns.

A local haulage firm, St Mary's Transport, occupied part of the disused Victoria Mills premises on School Lane for several years from 1948, the green livestock transporters becoming a familiar sight in Lubenham.

Overall, traffic on Britain's roads increased considerably from 1960s onwards putting pressure on the A427 which was an important east–west highway. After many years of campaigning the A14 from the Catthorpe interchange to Felixstowe finally opened in 1994 which relieved Lubenham of many heavy goods vehicles and much of the long distance traffic. As a result, the A427 was reclassified and downgraded to the A4304.

Canals

The Grand Union Canal skirts the north-west edge of the parish in what is one of the most beautiful parts of this waterway. To the west, the steep sided wooded Laughton Hills form an attractive backdrop, whilst to the east there are sweeping views across the Welland valley.

This stretch of canal, opened in 1814, finally completed the much needed link between the Leicester Navigation, which ended at nearby Debdale Wharf, and the Grand Junction in Northamptonshire.

Lubenham wharf near Bridge 57 at Bunker's Hill on the Laughton road was still in use in 1930s. Local farmers recall heavy goods such as coal and gravel being brought by barge, transferred to wagons and taken to Lubenham. In the early 19th century this wharf became the centre of a dispute between rival coal producers.[2] Coal was traditionally carried south from Derbyshire and unloaded at Debdale and Bowden wharfs, but in 1822, 500 tons of cheaper coal were brought in from Staffordshire and unloaded at Lubenham. The final outcome of this confrontation is not known! Lubenham wharf has all but disappeared in the undergrowth at the side of the canal, although indentations in the adjoining field still show traces of where the cart track ran.

The rapid development of the railways from the 1830s onwards led to the demise of the canal system. Like the old turnpike roads, canals could not compete with this faster and more efficient method of transport. Even bulk goods disappeared from the waterways and by the middle of the 20th century many of the canals had become derelict. The Grand Union Canal was nationalised in 1948,

Go with the flow: a crane appreciates the tranquility by Bridge 54.

Getting Around

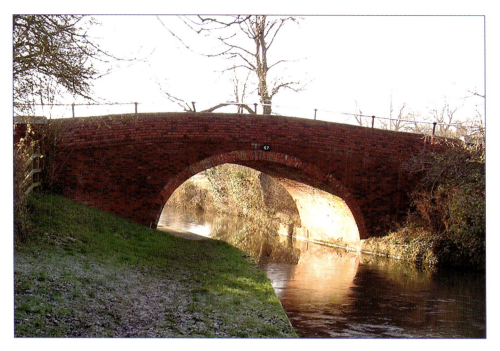

Canal Bridge 57. Lubenham Wharf was situated immediately beyond the bridge.

control transferring to the British Transport Commission, and in 1962 to the British Waterways Board, later British Waterways. Commercial traffic continued to decline, effectively ceasing in the 1970s. However, the transformation in recent years for recreational rather than commercial use means that canal boats, walkers, cyclists and people fishing are regularly using the stretch of waterway in Lubenham parish.

The popular tourist attraction of Foxton Locks lies just across the parish boundary. Opened in 1814, the ten locks, consisting of two staircases of five, raise boats up a 75ft steep incline. Alongside are the remains of the Foxton Inclined Plane. Powered by a stationary steam engine, boats were raised and lowered in two balanced caissons or tanks, so bypassing the system of locks. Opened in 1900, it remained fully operational for only ten years. Plans are underway to restore this Scheduled Ancient Monument.

Roger Wild

A passenger train at Lubenham Station in 1959.

The railway in Lubenham

Wednesday 30th August 1869 was an important day in Lubenham. After years of petitioning, the long awaited railway station finally opened. A report in *The Market Harborough Advertiser* of September 7th records the celebrations:

'On Wednesday last, through the generosity of some of the proprietors, and the public spirit of the vicar, the Rev. H.E. Bullivant, the opening of the New Station in this improving village, was celebrated by a large party of adults and school children paying a visit to Burleigh House by Stamford, where by kind permission of the Marquis of Exeter, they were allowed to see the beauties of the house, and to hold a picnic in the park. Wells' drum and fife band enlivened the occasion and the manager of the London and North Western Railway issued special tickets for the trip.'

The building of the line itself, which opened in 1850, must have had considerable impact on the life of this small rural community. Embankments and bridges were constructed, footpaths and bridleways diverted and the river Welland straightened as the track carved its way around the edge of the village, at one point passing within 100 yards of All Saints Church.

The line from Rugby to Stamford was a somewhat speculative route, designed to serve the need of the local communities but with the hope that it would attract the lucrative trade from the West Midlands to the East coast. Unfortunately, it never really succeeded as other routes took most of the trade and it is hard to conceive how this line ever made a serious profit. In July 1846, just one month after permission was granted in an Act of Parliament, the Rugby & Stamford merged with several other companies to form the London and North West Railway. It had become a small cog in a very large wheel.

Getting Around

The route ran 34 miles 7 furlongs and 2 chains from Rugby to join the Syston to Peterborough line near Stamford. Fortunately, details of the owners of the land affected in the parish have been preserved in the *Rugby-Stamford Railway Book of Reference 1846*.[3] Started in May 1847, it opened for passenger services three years later.

Although built some 19 years after the line itself, Lubenham was typical of the stations found along this route. The grand and often opulent buildings, designed to show off the status of the Railway Company and impress would-be investors, did not apply here. This was a small, relatively unimportant line, built in the more prudent days following the years of Railway Mania. Station design was standardised. The buildings were modular components built in Crewe by LNWR to a basic pattern. Although varying in size, they were made of brick and wood, with horizontal timber boarding and a flat roof which projected over the platform with canopies on three sides. A decorative valance supported by ornate cast-iron brackets provided the finishing touch.

Lubenham station was situated on an embankment to the west of the village. Originally there was one platform on the west side, although a shelter was not erected until 1872. When the railway was widened to two tracks in 1878, a booking office and waiting room were constructed on the platform nearest the village.

Each station was defined for different uses and the *1883 Railway Clearing House Handbook* listed Lubenham as being used for goods, passengers and parcels, furniture vans, livestock and horse boxes. Passenger timetables, published regularly in local newspapers such as the *Market Harborough Advertiser*, reveal that there were

Lubenham Station was built to a basic pattern by the London and North West Railway, using modular components made in Crewe.

RUGBY CO-OPERATIVE SOCIETY

Cheap Excursion on Bank Holiday.

ARRANGEMENTS have been made with the L. & N. W. Rly Co., for a SPECIAL EXPRESS TRAIN from Market Harborough and Rugby, calling at intermediate Stations and Brinklow, to

MORECAMBE BAY,

And LANCASTER and back, for 1, 2, 3, 4, 5, or 6 days

On MONDAY, August the 7th, 1882

TIMES OF STARTING AND FARES THERE AND BACK

Stations.	a.m.	1 day	2,3,4,5,or 6 days
Market Harborough..............	3.0		
Lubenham..........................	3.7		
Theddingworth...................	3.13		
Welford............................	3.21	5/6	8/-
Yelvertoft	3.31		
Lilbourne	3.36		
Clifton Mill	3.41		
RUGBY	3.45	5/-	7/6
Brinklow	3.50		

Arriving at Lancaster about 8.0 a.m., and Morecambe (Poulton Lane) about 8.10 a.m., giving Eleven hours at the Seaside. Children under 12, half-price.

The Return Train will leave Morecambe (Poulton Lane) the same day at 7.15 and Lancaster 7.30 p.m., and will be due at Rugby at 11.25 p.m., and Market Harborough at 12.10 p.m. Long-date Ticket Holders can return by ordinary trains any day during the week ending August 12th, 1882.

A.L.Mumford Esq. has kindly consented for the Rugby Steam Shed Whistle to be blown at 2.30 and 3.0 a.m., to arouse Excursionists.
TICKETS can be had at the office of the Society, 45, Chapel Street, Rugby; of Mr. ELAND, Printer, Market Harborough; of the Booking Clerk, Welford and Kilworth Station; and of Mr. WOODWARD, of Brinklow, up to 8 p.m. on Friday, August 4th. All tickets sold after 8 o'clock p.m. on August 4th, will be charged One Shilling extra. They can also be obtained by Post. An early application is necessary as only a limited number are ordered.

No ticket can be obtained at Rugby Station,
And no Tickets will be sold, under any circumstances, after 10 p.m. on Saturday, August 5th.

The Coffee Tavern at the Rugby Station will be open for Refreshments on the morning of the Excursion.

A Bank Holiday rail excursion to Morecambe Bay in 1882: A day return cost 5s 6d (when average earnings for a general labourer were only £1 a week). It was an early start from Lubenham but hardy travellers did get 11 hours at the Lancashire coast. London & North Western trains terminated at Morecambe Euston Road station, which closed in 1963 – three years before Lubenham station's own demise.

Getting Around

few trains calling at Lubenham. George Bradshaw's *Railway Guide* of 1887 listed four a day from Rugby and five in the other direction with one each way on Sundays. A similar entry in 1961 shows seven trains a day from Rugby and six from Peterborough stopped at Lubenham.

Whilst passenger services were a boon to this rural community, equally important, if not more so, was the use of Lubenham station for goods traffic. Bulky items such as building materials, road stone and coal were conveyed by rail with both a coal merchant and weighbridge situated just inside the entrance to the goods yard. Local farmers especially benefited as items such as machinery, fertiliser, seed and animal feed were brought in and farm produce, corn, potatoes, hay and other crops were dispatched to buyers and merchants. Many living in the village remember when the paddock next to the railway yard was crammed with cattle which had been brought in from Ireland and Wales for fattening on the lush grass of the Welland valley. In the autumn, fat cattle were sent in wagons to London and other markets.

Lubenham station was at its busiest during and just after the Second World War when service personnel were stationed at Papillon Hall and the nearby Airfield. In the late 1940s and 1950s the latter was used to store surplus army trucks and other equipment which were waiting for sale or dispersal. Lubenham was the nearest station and convoys of lorries, sometimes as many as four or five being towed by one vehicle, would wend their way through the village and along the Foxton Road.

The closure of the line came in 1966 when the last passenger train left Rugby at

End of the line: Dr Beeching's axe led to the station's closure in 1966 and subsequent demolition.
Right: A ticket for the last train to stop at Lubenham.

23

8.52pm on 6th June, the crew apparently having to spend over 20 minutes signing tickets before the train could leave the station. Like so many others, the Rugby to Peterborough line had become a victim of the Beeching Report.[4] The great hope of its designers and financial backers in the 1840s of capturing the lucrative east–west traffic never materialised. It was and remained a rural route providing a much needed service to local communities but, unable to make substantial profits, its demise was inevitable. Lubenham station was dismantled soon after it closed and the track removed in the late 1960s. The low bridge across the main road, always a traffic hazard, was demolished in 1972.

References
[1] Cossons, Arthur. *The Turnpike Roads of Leicestershire and Rutland*. Kairos Press, 2003.
[2] Stevens, Philip A. *The Leicester Line*. David & Charles, 1972.
[3] Rugby and Stamford Railway Book of Reference, 1846.
[4] The Reshaping of British Railways: Report by Dr Beeching, 1963.

Robbery
The 1967 film *Robbery* was partly shot on the railway line and bridge over the Theddingworth to Gumley Road. Starring Stanley Baker, the film was a dramatisation of the 1963 Great Train Robbery.

Church & Chapel

3. Church and Chapel

All Saints Church lies on the south side of the village near the river. A Grade 1 listed building, constructed of ironstone dressed with limestone, it was described by Nikolaus Pevsner, the noted architectural historian, as 'a delightfully unrestored building with a complex history'.[1] First mentioned in accounts in 1109 when Robert of Foxton gave the church and tithes to St Augustine Priory in Daventry, the earliest part of the present building dates from the end of the 12th century. It is almost certain that this replaced an earlier, possibly wooden, structure.

All Saints, 2002.

The chancel and nave were built between 1180 and 1215 during the Transition period between Romanesque and Gothic architecture with the north aisle and north and south chapels added about five years later. The original doorway and two pillars between the nave and the north aisle still survive. One arch in the north chapel is rounded, reflecting the Romanesque style introduced by the Normans. Often arches and pillars from this period were adorned with zigzag patterns or naturalist features such as leaves, humans or beasts and a fine example can be seen on the capital of one pillar where three grotesque faces, possibly symbolising Jack-in-the-Green or the Green Man, stare down from a surround of carved leaves.

The Green Man
Simple carvings depict a man's face peering out of dense foliage, often with branches or vines sprouting from the nose or mouth. A pre-Christian relic, it is usually interpreted as a symbol of re-birth, representing the cycle of growth each Spring.

The pointed Gothic arch leading to the north aisle was an engineering innovation at the time allowing the weight of the building to rest on a series of piers, shafts and ribs rather than thick load-bearing walls.

During the next century All Saints took on the appearance we find today. A bell tower built in 1250 is believed to have had a spire which blew down in the Great Storm of 1703.

Also in the mid 13th century the chancel arch was rebuilt, the north aisle widened and a south aisle erected. In order to allow more light after these alterations, a clerestory (the upper storey of the nave walls above the aisles) was constructed with three squared windows on either side, of which only four remain. The chancel was extended in the first half of the 14th century and the south chapel was demolished.

It is likely that the north and possibly the south chapels were chantries, privately endowed chapels where priests were paid to offer prayers for those who had built them. Around 1300, two niches were made in the wall of the north chapel. One contained the piscina or basin used for washing the communion vessels, whilst the second may have been a seat for the priest. A decorated squint or hagioscope in the north chapel allowed the chantry priest to follow the communion taking place at the high altar.

An important part of any mediaeval church was the rood, carved figures of Jesus on the Cross with the Virgin Mary and St John on either side, beneath which would be the rood screen that separated the chancel and altar from the nave and congregation. All Saints also had a rood loft or gallery which housed the choir and musicians; remains of the entrance to this loft can still be seen.

Although a painting of the Trinity Diagram had been uncovered in 1862, a significant discovery was made in 1989 during major restoration work when sections of mediaeval wall paintings were discovered hidden beneath layers of whitewash, relating to a time when parish churches were brightly painted and packed with images of Jesus, Mary and the Saints. The rose and the lily, especially the heraldic version

Church & Chapel

Left: These mediaeval wall paintings were discovered beneath layers of whitewash during major renovation work in 1989.
Above: The minstrel's gallery which replaced the rood loft.

of the fleur de lys, were common symbols of Mary. Could the painting to the right of the chancel arch show part of a fleur de lys and does the face behind the pulpit depict the Virgin Mary or, as Simon Jenkins believes[2], the head of an angel?

Monumental changes took place in the Church in England during the Reformation of the 16th century. Images of Mary and the Saints, wall paintings, statues and chantry chapels began to disappear as the teachings of Martin Luther and others proclaimed that entry to the Kingdom of Heaven was by faith alone and not through outward symbol of ceremony and ritual. Henry VIII's Act of Supremacy severed links with Rome, monasteries were dissolved and shrines and chantries forbidden. However, it was during the short reign of Edward VI that the

27

major changes took place in parish churches with the introduction of the Bible in English and the Book of Common Prayer which, for the first time, invited the congregation to pray with the minister and not separately. A wooden communion table replaced the altar and the priest became a minister (Latin for servant).

Under Elizabeth I stained glass windows, statues, roods and rood screens were removed or defaced and wall paintings whitewashed. The transformation from the old religion was not sudden, taking more than a quarter of a century to complete. Any Catholic icons which did remain were finally destroyed by Cromwell.

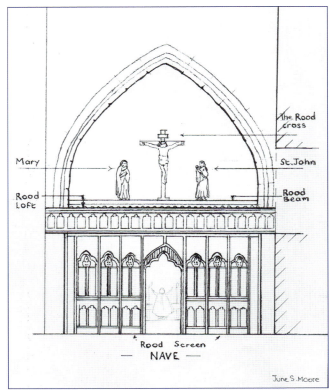

Above: A drawing of a typical rood screen, once a feature of All Saints. Many such screens were pulled down during the reign of Elizabeth I.

In All Saints the rood figures and screen were pulled down, the mediaeval stone altar replaced by a small wooden communion table and the walls whitewashed. The Royal Coat of Arms, symbol of the new church, supplanted the rood. A minstrel's gallery at the back of the nave which replaced the rood loft was removed in 1898.

Furniture and fittings

Unfortunately, in 2004 the wooden communion table which replaced the mediaeval altar was stolen from the north chapel, now the vestry. The present 17th century altar and the sanctuary chair came from the Old Hall. There is a popular story that this chair was used by Charles I when he stayed at the Old Hall before the Battle of Naseby in 1645. An oak chest in the north chapel formerly contained the vestments, chalice and parish registers dating back to 1559.

The origins of the two-decker pulpit with tester or sounding board are uncertain. The upper part may date from 1620 with the tester, lower part and steps from 1747. However another source implies that the whole structure was put in at the same time as the box pews in 1810–1812. The box pews are rare; only around 140 examples still exist in England.

Church & Chapel

Above: The interior of All Saints Church, 2005. **Below:** a photograph taken by the Rev W. Law on 4 August 1856. Note the cottage (now the Tower House) in the background before the major alterations of 1862.

Left: The Bullivant Memorial. **Right:** The stained glass window in the south aisle, installed in 1947 in memory of Captain George Wernher who was killed in action in 1942. **Below:** All Saints in the snow. The dry stone wall was rebuilt by volunteers in 2000–2002.

The mediaeval stone font damaged during the 1810 alterations was replaced by the present carved structure. Work in 1950 to fit new oak choir stalls led to the discovery of sections of the rood screen and a 14th century aumbry, a small cupboard or recess in the wall.

The present organ, built by public subscription, was installed in 1872.

Church & Chapel

> **All Saints Church wall hanging by Linda Straw, commissioned by June Moore.**
>
> Linda Straw is an internationally known quilter who employs a technique she developed which combines appliqué, quilting and embroidery using a sewing machine. This method, now known by her name, is widely taught in workshops and City & Guilds and was introduced to Europe and America over the last decade. Great stress is placed on design and it is her interest in literature, art and history which makes her work unusual. She has appeared in many publications and her workshops are held not only in Britain and Ireland but in Europe and the United States.
>
> Working to commission or for exhibition she has gained much acclaim with such pieces as the huge 'Millennium Tapestry', '1588 and All That' and 'Romeo and Juliet'. In 2004 she won first prize at the Festival of Quilts in Birmingham.
>
> The All Saint tapestry depicts many of the locals going about their daily life, and often records their contribution to the village, be it as a bellringer or helping with events such as the Scarecrow Weekend.

There are two stained glass windows of note in the church. One, depicting Christ and the four Evangelists, is dedicated to the memory of Joshua and Jane Perkins, farmers and manufacturers in the 19th century. The second, installed in 1947, is in honour of Capt. George (Alex) Wernher, killed in action in North Africa in 1942. His family lived at Thorpe Lubenham Hall.

The church bells are rung regularly. The tenor bell dates from 1624, three bells were recast in 1724 and a fifth added. A sixth bell was purchased in 2001 following fund-raising in the village.

The churchyard contains several interesting gravestones, including one which dates from 1689 and others from the 1720s.

All Saints continues to play a central part in the life of Lubenham as it has done for centuries. Fund raising, especially towards the upkeep of this historic building, takes place regularly and in 2001–2 the dry stone wall around the churchyard was rebuilt by volunteers from the village.

Independent and Congregational Chapel

On April 12th 1830 John Ellson, a butcher from Lubenham, donated a parcel of land for use by Independent Dissenters in the area and a Board of Trustees was established to raise the necessary funds to build a chapel.

The former Congregational Chapel on Main Street.

There had been a history of Nonconformity, or refusal to accept or conform to the doctrines of the Church of England, in the village. In 1672 John Shuttleworth was licensed to preach at Lubenham and use his house as a meeting place, and similar licences were granted to others in subsequent years. By the beginning of the 18th century there were reportedly 20 Independents and 10 Baptists in Lubenham.

The foundation stone was laid in November 1837. The chapel was built of corrugated iron, a new material at the time, at a cost of £220. The first service was held in the following year, on November 28th. However, the building soon became too small and was demolished in 1877 to be replaced by the present larger brick structure.

John Benjamin Haddon of Lubenham Lodge was a particularly generous benefactor. In 1879 he and his wife donated a communion service consisting of a nickel silver cup and two plates which were supplied by the Lubenham firm of Eli Rimmington & Son. A year later Haddon bequeathed £400 (approximately £30,000 in today's figures) to the Trustees to be invested in government stock for the benefit of the chapel.

As the congregation decreased the Chapel ceased to be a place of worship in 1987 and is now used for commercial purposes.

References

[1] Pevsner, Nikolaus. *Leicestershire and Rutland*. Yale University Press, reprinted 2002.
[2] Jenkins, Simon. *England's Thousand Best Churches*. Penguin Books, 1999.

4. School days - education and learning

When the present school building officially opened at Easter 1859 there was no national system for schools and education was neither free nor compulsory.

Early history

Details of how and indeed if the children of Lubenham were educated before the 19th century are scarce and a matter of conjecture. In the Middle Ages the wealthy were taught by private tutors or in public schools. Education for others was mainly in the hands of the clergy and religious establishments so any basic instruction in reading or writing would have come from local priests, many of whom were barely literate themselves. During Tudor and Stuart times there was a burgeoning of grammar schools, often funded by wealthy merchants and traders, such as that founded by Robert Smyth in Market Harborough in 1607 for the education of 24 boys from Harborough and the Welland Valley. At the same time the need for apprentices to be more skilled and literate led to the establishment of schools run by various Guilds. There is no record of boys from Lubenham being educated in this way. However, there is written evidence that by 1630 Jonathan Deverex, curate of Lubenham, used the North Chapel (now the vestry) of All Saints Church as a school room, a practice which continued on and off for 200 years.

All Saints Church of England Primary School in 2006.

By the early 19th century big changes were taking place in education nationally. Organisations such as The National Society made grants of money to both day and Sunday schools. Lubenham was recognised in 1815 and by 1819, 70 boys and 31 girls attended, with boys still educated in the North Chapel and girls elsewhere, perhaps in a different part of the church. There is also evidence of another school in the village at this time. Described as 'The Private Academy of Thomas Eldridge', it opened in 1832. Few facts are known or when it closed but by 1835 it had ten pupils, three boys and seven girls.

Opening of the National School Building

The process of erecting a new school building to replace the Parish School in the Church began at a Vestry Meeting in January 1857. A committee made up of 'the great and the good' of the village was established to raise the necessary funds and obtain a suitable site. By September 1858 they had obtained three-quarters of the £1000 required from a parliamentary grant, the National Society and the Poor Law Board. The rest of the money was raised through subscription.

Advertisement from Schools Guardian, 27th July 1889

WANTED (September), a certified MASTER, a SEWING MISTRESS and ASSISTANT TEACHER. Communicant, organ, choir and Sunday School.

Joint salary £140, with nice house and good garden. Railway station.

Address: The Vicar, Lubenham, Market Harborough.

Copy in School Manager's Minute Book 1889, held in Record Office for Leicestershire, Leicester and Rutland.

School Days

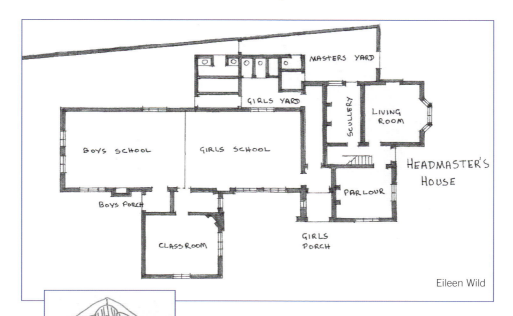

Eileen Wild

Above: The original layout of the school, with the Headmaster's house and Master's Yard.

Left: A drawing of the original plaque for the National School.

Below: The new school hall, opened in 2006.

35

> *Jan 18:* Great storm of wind and snow from the east. Several plates blown from the ridge. Back door blown to and split. Pump frozen.
>
> *Jan 19:* Storm continued unabated during the night. Up at 6a.m. to dig way through the snow and light the school fires. Only 10 present.
>
> *Extract from Lubenham School Log 1881*

The school was designed by architect J. Cranston of Birmingham, in the Gothic Revival style of red brick with decorated patterns in blue brick and Northampton-shire stone arches over the doors and windows. It had a slate roof and tall chimneys which have since been reduced in height. The original plaque for the National and Parochial School on the front of the building was replaced by a clock costing 40 guineas, the legacy of Mr J.B. Smith.

Inside, the large room (60 x 20 feet and open to the roof) was designed for 200 children and separated between boys and girls. This has since been divided into two rooms. There was also a smaller classroom (18 x 16 feet). The adjoining Master's House was later incorporated into the main school.

Several alterations were made in 20th century, including an extension added to the rear in the 1960s. A new school hall, designed to be in keeping with the original building, was opened in 2006.

School life in the 19th century

The Education Act of 1870 substantially changed education in England and Wales. The country was divided into School Districts, and School Boards were elected. These Boards were responsible for raising sufficient funds to maintain the school, guarantee the attendance of all children between the ages of five and 13, and appoint officers to enforce this. However, school attendance was not made obligatory until 1876 and elementary education was not effectively free until 1891. School Boards could charge a weekly fee up to 9d but as Lubenham was established as a charity school in 1815 children of the poor were never charged more than 2d, still substantial when the average weekly wage for a labourer at this time was £1 to £1.10s and less for those working in agriculture.

Subjects taught were religious education, reading, writing, arithmetic, grammar, geography, history, sewing and cutting out, singing, music and drill. The amount of money given to the school depended on the annual Inspector's Report. For example, that of 1873 said 'the state of the school shows marked improvement' and a grant of £50.5s was awarded.

The summary of the Inspector's Report of 10th April 1889 stated that 'arithmetic was very weak in upper standards and spelling in 2nd standard. Needlework deserved praise except in 2nd standard where it was poor. Singing by note was good'. The number presented for the annual examination was 75 with 68 passes in reading, 63 in writing, 40 in arithmetic, giving a total of 171 passes. The government grant was £63.4s.8d.

Lubenham School registers for the time make fascinating reading. The earliest, dating from 1855, reveals the school was attended by children between the ages of three and 13 and contains many family names still present in the village today.

School Days

Above: With a bit of imagination you can just about make out Mr and Mrs C.J. Perry with their daughter Florence and the infants class of 1903–04.

Below: Lubenham School circa 1907.
Back row, left to right: ?, A. Barker, R. Ashton, L. Cooper, R. Petty, H. Newman, A. Mitchell; middle row: M. Cooper, G. Ireland, W. Robinson, E. Mutton, N. Timson, W. Loomes, E. Gayton; third row: A. Jordan, F. Coleman, E. Coleman, W. Carter, M. Newman, ?, C. Underwood. G. Ireland, ?; front row: ?, M. Partridge, J. Cooper, ?, L. Goode, L. Gayton, J. Carter.

School holidays were half days and corresponded with religious festivals such as Ascension Day, although two and a half days were allowed after Easter and one week at Christmas. School continued throughout the summer, except during harvest when children were expected to help with the work. Absence through sickness was more noticeable in winter and there were several occasions when the school closed for two weeks or more 'on account of scarlet fever being prevalent in the village'.[1]

Above: The class of 1910.
Below: Lubenham School gardening lessons 1922–3. Left to right: L. Saunders, A. Harris, F. Hubbard (?), Ron Ashton, W. Payne, Geoff York (?), – Tomkins, Reg Cockerill, headteacher Mrs Butler, Eric Butler, N. Wilson, – Liquorice.

School Days

Sometimes teachers decided to shut the school for their own convenience. In 1856, for instance, the children were given three half-day holidays so that teachers could attend Rockingham Horticultural Show, Rockingham Flower Show and a missionary meeting in Harborough Church!

Education in the 20th century and beyond

Following the Education Act of 1902 schools became the responsibility of County Councils and managers replaced the School Boards. Twenty-four years later, schools were again reorganised, this time into primary (up to the age of 11) and modern, including existing grammar and technical schools. The fact that the older children from the village were to attend schools in Market Harborough caused consternation amongst the parents and there were protests to the Education Committee. A resolution was proposed that

> *'this meeting of parishioners of Lubenham protests at the children over 11 years of age going to Market Harborough on account of the distance, danger of 2 miles on a main road and whether suitable arrangements for food and clothes as well as the extra expense entailing on the agricultural labourer'.*

The resolution was rejected and the reforms went ahead.

The Manager's Minute Books imply that, unlike today's school governors whose main concerns are finance, curriculum and policy, managers were more pre-occupied with the mundane: the appointment of a cleaner, cutting down of trees and the condition of the boiler. Even during World War II there were few references to the evacuees who almost doubled the school population and no mention made to their number, where they came from or where they were taught.

A retirement presentation to Headteacher Miss Batty in 1960. Denise Leeder, the youngest pupil, presents a bouquet whilst the Rev B. Peake looks on.

Miss Batty would arrive each day on her sit-up-and-beg bicycle with a suitcase strapped on the carrier behind her. She always looked a typical school mistress – quite prim with her hair tied in a bun. She was a very strict but fair teacher, immensely proud of her school, and consequently highly respected and loved.
My memory is of a very happy school and Miss Batty was a real credit to it.

Miss Batty as remembered by former pupil Margaret Bale (née Woolmer)

Lubenham School around 1963–4: *Back row:* Philip Murray, Neil Davies, Norman Holton, Trevor Crook, Trevor Jones, Mervyn Leeder, Jeffrey Irving.
Middle row: Kathleen Howard, Jennifer Jones, Linda Loakes, Stephanie Maddever, Wendy Crook, Gillian Fox.
Front row: Maureen Rees, Catherine Murray, Elizabeth Hailstone (?), Linda Coleman, Kay Taylor, Janet Saunders, Elizabeth Mayben.
The dog belonged to the teacher Mrs Bowley.

Later reforms in the 20th century saw the re-organisation of secondary education. The 1944 Education Act led to the tripartite system of grammar, technical and modern and the introduction of the 11+ exam. It also ended fee paying in state secondary schools. Some 15 years later, Leicestershire began introducing a system of comprehensive education in which secondary schools were re-organised into High Schools (11–14 years) and Upper Schools (14-plus). Whilst these changes did not directly involve Lubenham School, they did affect the lives of children from the village.

Lubenham All Saints Primary is a dynamic, well-regarded school and in 2011 had 81 pupils and seven teachers.

Reference
[1] *Lubenham School Manager's Minute Books*

5. Mansions and cottages

Lubenham has an eclectic mixture of houses, reflecting the economic and social history of the village. These range from country mansions to small family homes, thatched cottages to Victorian terraces and modern 20th century properties.

Significant buildings still survive, witness to the past and present prosperity of the area, although some like Papillon Hall have been demolished and others, most notably the Old Hall and Thorpe Lubenham Hall, have been greatly altered or reduced in size. Distinctive properties in the heart of the village demonstrate Lubenham's long association with horses and hunting. The unusual number of medium sized houses dating from the 17th century onwards is probably the result of the early enclosures and the large proportion of freeholders in the village at that period. Many of these houses were remodelled or rebuilt in brick during the 18th century and most of the thatched roofs were later replaced by slate. Victorian buildings and small housing developments added in the last hundred years create a blend of styles, old and new.

The Old Hall

The Old Hall is the oldest vernacular building in the village. Although a manor in Lubenham can be traced back to Domesday, little is known about the buildings. Records show that a manor house, Baud's Manor, existed here from at least the 14th century and probably earlier. There are no details about its size or appearance, although evidence from a later building may give some clues. It is almost certain

Above: A drawing of The Old Hall before demolition, c.1774 Nichols.[1]
Below: The Old Hall, taken by the Rev W. Law. The photograph is dated 1893 but the first plate was probably made about 30 years before, in the early 1860s.
Bottom: The Old Hall in 2012.

that the Old Hall, as Baud's Manor became known, was rebuilt or re-modelled in Elizabethan times on this former, possibly timber-framed, mediaeval structure. Roof timbers in the part which still remains have been dated to the 1300s, indicating it was once part of the earlier construction.

Records show that the later 16th century house was H-shaped in plan, two storeys with no attics and surrounded by a moat, part of which still remains as a scheduled Ancient Monument. Internal features such as a large hall, possible

> **Solar:** A room smaller than the Great Hall which afforded greater privacy to the Lord of the Manor and his family. This was a room of comfort and status and usually included a fireplace, decorated woodwork, tapestries and wall hangings.

solar and kitchen complex are typical of a mediaeval manor. However, by 1774 the Old Hall had fallen into disrepair and much of the house was demolished, leaving only the south wing which can be seen today. A contemporary drawing and detailed description of the Old Hall before it was partially pulled down can be found in *The History and Antiquities of the County of Leicestershire*, dated 1798.

The remaining part of this Grade II listed building was extensively refurbished in the late 20th century.

Kitchen complex in a mediaeval manor house

Kitchen: including ovens for baking and large fireplaces for smoking and roasting food.

Buttery: room for storing and dispensing beverages, usually ale.

Pantry: room for storing perishable food.

Storerooms: for non-perishable kitchen items and products.

Papillon Hall

About a mile to the west of Lubenham is the site of one of the most fascinating and enigmatic houses in the parish. Constructed around 1624 for David Papillon, the Hall reflected the owner's background in military engineering. Built rather like a fort and surrounded by a moat, it stood on a spur of land above the flood plain of the Welland and commanded 360 degree views of the adjacent countryside. Several natural springs ensured a continuous supply of water.

A drawing of Papillon Hall by Nichols.[1]

The Hall was octagonal in shape, built of stone with only one door and large, strong windows. All the rooms on the first floor were interconnected. Four attics on the top floor had sloping sides within the gables, which created a cross-shaped roof, with the flat parts between coated with lead, giving rise to the theory that these areas were intended to carry cannon. Each attic was different in design, with that on the east side being particularly strange. The en-

Above: A postcard of Papillon Hall in 1903, taken from the south east.
Below: Remains of the lily pond in 2008.

trance was so low that it was only accessible by crawling on hands and knees.

In 1903 the Hall was bought by Frank Bellville, who commissioned Sir Edwin Lutyens to redesign the house, with gardens attributed to Gertrude Jekyll. Incorporating the old hall, Lutyens added four new wings to create a butterfly shape, no doubt inspired by the name Papillon, which is French for butterfly.

He added additional bedroom space by raising the roof and creating a third floor. The new wings accommodated a drawing room, billiard room, dining room and kitchen and servant's hall with pantry and cellar. Contemporary photographs show this to be a very attractive house but the high cost of maintenance and its occupation during World War II by British and American servicemen led to its demise and it was pulled down in the early 1950s. All that survive are remains of the lily pond, greenhouse, summer house and stables. It is almost inconceivable that a Lutyens house would be demolished today.

Thorpe Lubenham Hall

Although situated across the river in Northamptonshire, the Hall's proximity and close historic ties means that it is considered an integral part of the village. The original manor house is believed to have stood on an island surrounded by a moat not far from the present hall, although its structure and appearance are unknown. The credibility of a 1797 engraving in Nichols [1] is now generally disputed as the position and aspect of the building as shown from the church cannot be accurate.

The present red brick Georgian house in the Queen Anne style probably replaced an earlier smaller structure on the site, a theory substantiated by the presence of an

The rear of the Hall in 2002.

The Hall in 1961 before the demolition of the West and Nursery wings.

old gable end incorporated into the later building. Constructed for F.P. Stratford around 1800 it became part of his 1400 acre estate which included parts of Farndon, Marston Trussell and the Laughton Hills.

In 1912 the Hall was sold to Gordon Cunard, a member of the shipping dynasty, and around eight years later was purchased by Sir Harold and Lady Zia Wernher. This was the start of a golden period for this substantial property, with 26 members of staff employed in the house and gardens. Improvements and renovations were made; a covered tennis court, golf course and polo field were constructed, now sadly all gone, and the Wernhers built up a stable of hunters, polo ponies and racehorses, the most famous Being Brown Jack (see Chapter 10, *Horses and hunting*).

The Hall was purchased in 1966 by Viscount Kemsley. The west and nursery wings were demolished during 1970s, reducing the house to half its original size.

In 1985 the estate was sold and the new owners have since added rooms to the east and altered the front aspect of the building.

Manor Farm
(The Green)

This is a fine Queen Anne house built at the beginning of the 18th century, constructed of brick with ashlared stone dressings. The west front, two storeys with attics, retains its period sash windows with thick glazing bars, although the central six-panel door and roof dormers are 20th century. Attached on the north side is a brick barn with a Swithland slate roof. Manor Farm became the home of the Lord of the Manor when John Wright moved from the dilapidated Old Hall at the end of the 18th century.

The Laurels
(Main Street)

The Laurels in the early 20th century.

Also known as *Parva Sed Apta* (translated as Small but Comfortable), this was built around 1850 for Joshua Perkins, a local businessman and factory owner. Costing around £20,000 (£1.5m in today's figures) it reflects the growing prosperity and confidence of Victorian Britain. Constructed of brick with slate roof, this imposing two-storey house, currently used as offices, has steps leading to a central doorway with impressive bay windows either side. It contains a number of interesting internal features including a roof lantern to give light to the entrance hall. The property with its once extensive garden complete with ha-ha, is separated from the main road by a decorative cast iron fence. The gardens contained a Victorian ice-house where ice was packed under a hollow stone floor. The adjoining building is believed to be the former coach house, although this interpretation is not certain. The original stable block for 12 horses was situated further to the west along Main Street and has since been converted to commercial premises.

Farms and freeholds – medium size houses from the 17th Century onwards

Records show that from the 17th century onwards Lubenham had an unusually large number of freeholders with small estates. This can partly be explained by the break-up of the Baud–Wolwardington manor in the 15th century and the early enclosures of 1600–1601. At the beginning of the 17th Century there were 30 farms in the village, of which 17 belonged to independent freeholders. The remaining enclosures took place following an Act of Parliament in 1766. As a result there are several medium sized houses dating from this period which still survive today.

Eden House
(Church Walk)

Eden House is a cruck beamed A-frame house (an A frame supports the roof independently from the walls) dating from around 1580. Built of stone and brick, the exposed box frame timbers are clearly visible on the south front. A date of 1731 in the brickwork shows that an extension was added to the right of the original two bays during 18th century. There is an outhouse of brick with plain tile roof, possibly a former dairy, from the same period. Further alterations took place during the following 200 years including the addition of three gable dormers. Internally there are exposed beams and joists, although most of the partition walls have been removed.

Verger's Cottage
(Church Walk)

Verger's Cottage is a beautiful 18th century house with Flemish bond brickwork and fine old oak studded door. Previously thatched, there is a date mark IW 1737 in brick on the west wall. The north elevation has a single storey stone porch, probably 19th century. There are early references to the interior as having a bressumer or large beam supported on an early 17th century bracket with strap work carving.

The Old Vicarage
(23 The Green)

The house was only used as a vicarage from the 19th century until it was sold in the 1980s. Constructed of brick and stone, it dates in part to 17th century. Despite many alterations and additions there is still evidence of the original building, most notably stone jambs which were part of the original mullioned windows, a single light window in the upper floor and the right bay of dressed stone on the south front. Internally, one ceiling has a carved wooden beam from around 1500, thought to be ecclesiastical in origin.

The Old Vicarage in the 1950s.

Dower House
(14 Rushes Lane)

Formerly known as Figpeth, the Dower House originates from the late 18th Century. It is two and a half

storeys high, constructed in brick with 19th and 20th century alterations including a concrete tile roof. The date 1776 is incorporated in the south gable wall in burnt headers, the last figure obscured by the insertion of a single 20th century casement window.

Attached is a three-storey brick cottage of similar date, the upper floor being added in 1800s, which was the Stud Groom's cottage when both these properties belonged to the Cottage Estate.

Rose Cottage
(1 The Green)

This very attractive brick and timber frame building is thought to date from c.1638 and renamed during the 18th century. The thatched roof has two gable chimney stacks, one of which is external. The rear elevation has visible 18th century close-studding with rendered infill on the first storey. Although the casement windows are later in date, the open latticed porch with canopy is 19th century.

The attached brick and slate tiled building was used as a butcher's shop from the 1800s until the 1960s. The pantiled area was formerly a slaughterhouse, later converted to a smithy. It still contains the old forge.

The Hollies
(Main Street)

The Hollies is another example of a medium sized property of this period. The thatched portion is believed to date from the early 18th century but similar brickwork in the east wall suggests that the main three-storey section was erected in the 19th century around an earlier structure. Internal features from both Georgian and Victorian times indicate several periods of expansion.

The Draper's House
(Main Street)

The Draper's House is a timber framed house which has been used as a shop for many years, including as Lubenham's last general store and post office. A carved bracket to the main ceiling beam is dated 1668 with the initials M.W.C. It is almost certain that this date refers to the whole structure.

Clockwise from top: The Draper's House today; as a general store and post office and as Collins store.

The White House
(corner of Main Street and School Lane)

The White House is a 17th century farmhouse that was rebuilt in the 18th century while preserving its earlier internal arrangements. The old beams can still be seen in the brickwork in School Lane. The thatched roof was replaced by slate in 1949. It was a working farm until the 1960s, the outbuildings previously housing the dairy, cow sheds and stables. As can be seen here, it has also served as a tea room.

Two other farmhouses of note are the 18th century Mill House on The Green, associated with the windmill on top of the hill behind, and Adam's Farm in Rushes Lane, a Georgian farmhouse and dairy with attached 19th century house.

Mansions & Cottages

The original stone wall is partially exposed on the south end of the painted exterior.

Two farmhouses in the parish may also have been built as a result of the 1600-01 enclosures.

An outbuilding at Holmes Farm on Foxton Road, surveyed in 2010, was found to have an early 17th century ironstone plinth with 18th century brick above. An upper storey was added in the mid 19th century.

Lubenham Lodge, formerly Kirby Lodge, dates from the 18th century. The house, on the Lubenham–Laughton road, has been considerably altered and renovated from 1932 onwards to create a substantial and attractive Queen Anne style country house overlooking the canal.

Houses associated with horses and hunting

Lubenham has a long association with horses and hunting, attracting wealthy families to the area, especially in the 19th century. One property that exemplifies this is The Tower House on Rushes Lane.

The Tower House
(Rushes Lane)

Formerly a Georgian farmhouse built in 1771 and named The Cottage, the Tower House was enlarged by Messrs Cubitt in 1862 as a hunting box for Jack 'Cherry' Angell.

Constructed of brick with stone dressings and slate roofs, the original house facing south towards the Church has a central doorway now flanked by 19th century bay windows and a date stone inscribed JC 1771 at first floor level. A 19th century extension to the west accommodates a large sitting room, once with a highly decorated ceiling, with two interesting bay windows, one

51

painted with Gothic tracery, the other polygonal with a painted arch above. When viewed from Rushes Lane this west elevation is rather plain with only two windows, one with a flat arch and another oriel with conical roof. The tower with its circular corbelled staircase turret was built in 1865, purportedly to allow Jack Angell to watch his horses training in nearby fields. Two large rooms and a conservatory on the east side were demolished probably after World War I.

The impressive double-sided stables dating from 1852 were converted into a workshop making lingerie in 1950. This closed following a disastrous fire in 2001 and the building subsequently transformed into five mews cottages.

> **Messrs Cubitt** were some of the most eminent builders of the 19th century, with major developments in Bloomsbury, Pimlico and Belgravia. A favourite of Queen Victoria, Thomas Cubitt built Osborne House on the Isle of Wight and the new east front of Buckingham Palace.

Gore Lodge
(1 School Lane)

Gore Lodge, originally built in the 1730s as a farmhouse, is a fine example of a 19th century hunting box which was extensively redesigned by the noted architect Robert W. Edis in 1875 for Jack Angell, owner of the Cottage Estate. Angell added the mock Tudor front, raised the roof to provide a second floor with attics and enlarged the living accommodation. Evidence of the alterations is shown by the blocked window with cambered arch and partially obscured date, 17?? in burnt headers on the east elevation.

> **A hunting box:** a house with stables usually used as a residence only during the hunting season.

> **The House That Jack Built:** Jack Angell paid for the extensive alterations to Gore Lodge after loosing a bet with the then owner, his uncle John Gore. As a result a new name, The House that Jack Built, was suggested. The inscription can still be seen on the porch above the door.
>
> Architect **Colonel Robert William Edis** was responsible for designing a number of high profile buildings in the 19th century, including additions to the royal residence at Sandringham, the Liverpool Street Railway hotel and the Grand Central Hotel in Marylebone.

Mansions & Cottages

Adjoining the house to the rear and behind a 2.5m high wall are the stable ranges, built of brick with Welsh slate roofs. There is also a cottage, Groom's Cottage, with distinctive ornamental facing tiles and a clock made by Rimmington of Lubenham.

Part of the former stable block.

Workers cottages from 17th century onwards

Although not immediately obvious, several cottages and small houses dating back three or four centuries still exist in Lubenham. Many have been incorporated into larger buildings or so altered externally that their origins and dates are not directly apparent. Piper's Piece on Main Street is one such example. Internal evidence of former doorways, staircases and a 3ft thick mud wall point to this once being three cottages, probably lace maker's dwellings, dating from the 1700s.

49 The Green

49 The Green was originally two cruck framed cottages dating from c.1600, making it one of the oldest houses in the village. However, its appearance was greatly altered in the early Victorian period when it was enlarged and the thatched roof replaced with slate.

The Old Bake House
(The Green)

The Old Bake House was originally two thatched cottages built in 17th century. The later bakery can be pinpointed by the door in the end wall at first floor level where flour was hauled up and stored. The bread oven is still *in situ* in the room below.

Other cottages from 1600s onwards have been demolished since World War II, either because they were in a dilapidated condition or to make way for new development.

The Old Bake House: note the door at first floor level.

One example is a row of cruck cottages on The Green c.1600 which had brick fronts but wattle and daub to the rear and mud side walls. The thatched roof had been covered in corrugated tin. The whole row had become unstable when it was demolished in 1970s. Houses built on Main Street in the 1930s to accommodate workers from Thorpe Lubenham Estate replaced two existing old dwellings and a row of small thatched and ivy-covered cottages in Rushes Lane was demolished by Harborough District Council to make way for a pair of semi-detached houses. A 1970s bungalow on the corner of Church Walk, which replaced a small thatched timber cottage with lath and daub infilling, is just one of many other examples which could be cited.

One of the cruck cottages on The Green

Victorian houses

Major alterations took place during the 19th century. Two brick houses for the station master and signalman were built when the railway station opening in 1869. Former farm worker's cottages at either end of the village are attractive examples of Victorian architecture.

Western Villa on Westland Close was a fine Victorian farmhouse which was demolished in the 1960s. Many of the buildings in the centre of the village dating from this period are associated with Victoria Mills, a large factory owned by Joshua Perkins and Sons.

Western Villa, now demolished.

54

20th century and beyond

Laughton Road in 1922.

The largest housing expansion in the village occurred during the first half of the 20th century. Council-owned properties were built along Foxton and Laughton Roads in 1922–1924 and the remainder on Foxton Road 11 years later. More were added after World War II on Paget Road, Main Street and School Lane. These provided much needed social housing, although the vast majority are now privately owned. Four 'Swedish' houses built of timber were erected on Westgate Lane in 1946 at a time of housing and materials shortage. All but one have since been demolished and replaced by brick-built bungalows. Six semi-detached houses on School Lane/Church Walk were built by Thorpe Lubenham Estate for their workers.

The next large programme took place in 1968–69 on the site of Western Villa when mainly semi-detached properties were built to house officers from the newly opened Gartree Prison. These are now privately owned.

Small developments of mainly detached houses have taken place since 1980s such as those in Tower Court, Acorn Close and behind the Mill House, and individual barn conversions and properties on smaller plots and gardens. So-called 'more affordable' housing has been built in Connell Close and The Hawthorns, on the site of the former garage on Main Street.

Above: The last of the four post-war 'Swedish' houses on Westgate Lane awaiting demolition. **Below:** One of the houses built behind Mill House.

Although the proximity of Market Harborough has often been of concern, Lubenham is a village which has avoided large scale housing development. However, the same is not true of the parish. When HMP Gartree opened in 1966 houses were built nearby to accommodate prison officers, but this estate, some two miles from Lubenham, has always struggled to become integrated into village life. In 2010 work started on the development of the Airfield Farm site

55

with the construction of commercial properties. Plans were also submitted to build up to 1000 houses. Development on this scale would more than double the population of the parish.

Reference

[1] Nichols, J. *The History and Antiquities of the County of Leicester,* volume II, part II, 1798.

Earning a Living

6. Earning a living: Employment through the ages

The traditional view of people not only living but working in a close-knit village community may be somewhat idealistic but is partially true. For centuries farming was the mainstay of Lubenham's economy. There were also small trades and enterprises such as shops and even employment in local factories, but by the 21st century things had changed considerably.

Agriculture

The open-field system which dominated rural life for decades developed during the late Saxon period and continued under the feudal structure of the Normans. Land was farmed communally, usually in a three-field crop rotation system, with much of the produce going in dues to the Lord of the Manor. A team of oxen ploughed the fields into narrow strips that were distributed so that each peasant farmer

The ridges and furrows of the open-field system can still be seen around Lubenham.

57

REFERENCE
to the Inclosures.

Tennants Names.	Letters Refering to the Mapp.	Names to the Fields or Closes.	Quality	Quantity		
				Acres	R.	Ps.
Iohn Barnes.	A.	*ye Manner Hall* Houses, Yards, Garden, and Orchard		1	1	33.
	B.	Little Home Close at old Orchard	Pasture	3	0	20.
	C.	Little Inhomes in Northamptonshire	Meadow	1	1	27.
	D.	Great Inhomes	Ditto	4	1	27.
	E.	Great Hall Close	Pasture	14	3	31.
	F.	Little Hall Close	Ditto	2	1	25
	G.	Monks Close	Meadow	5	0	03.
	H.	Apple Croft at Abtrow Croft Close	Pasture	7	1	23.
	I.	Pains Close	Ditto	32	2	15.
	K.	Broad Close	Meadow	37	1	20.
	L.	Northfield Meadow	Ditto	31	1	30.
	M.	The Northfield	Pasture	171	2	35.
	N.	Upper Northfield Meadow	Meadow	17	3	25.
	O.	The Midle Ditto	Ditto	12	1	20.
	P.	The Lower Ditto	Ditto	15	2	29.
		Totall.		359	1	19.
Thos Coleman.	Q.	Upper Foxon Hill	Pasture	9	2	21.
	R.	The Lower Ditto	Ditto	12	0	20.
		Totall.		21	3	09
Willm Allard.	S.	Scoborough field	Pasture	110	1	07.
	T.	First Scoborough Meadow	Meadow	8	3	06.
	V.	Second Ditto	Ditto	12	3	01.
	W.	Third Ditto	Ditto	17	3	20.
	X.	A Small plott in Northamptonshire				17
		Totall.		157	3	11.

Extract from Isaac Bermingham's survey of 1734.

Earning a Living

had an equal share of good and poor land. The heavy plough always turned the soil to the right, creating the undulating ridge and furrow landscape which can still be seen in fields around Lubenham today.

Villages became nucleated, a cluster of huts each with a small toft or garden in which to grow vegetables. As well as the open fields, other areas around the settlement were typically the demesne (land belonging to the lord), meadow, common land for grazing and forest or woodland.

Rural society changed in the years following the Black Death of 1348–50 when shortage of labour allowed peasants to demand higher wages. It led to the rise of the yeoman farmer. However, the open field system largely continued until the Enclosure Acts of the 18th Century. A survey in 1734 carried out by Isaac Bermingham for the then Lord of the Manor, Samuel Wright, details the situation in Lubenham:

The open field land belonging to Lubenham lies in three separate fields, distinguished by the names of the West, Middle and East Fields and are managed in such a manner that one field is always in fallow, another under wheat and barley and the third under beans and peas, and are rotated annually.

It is again divided into lands and leys, or ploughed ground and grass, which lies in furlongs which have proper names. The gleads, or low grounds, that run between the furlongs, and the common baulks that lie dispersed between the lands all over the fields, are called common or cott grass, because all persons who have a freehold in the open field have a right to a share in them, in proportion to the quantity of freehold land they own.

These gleads and baulks are their meadow ground which they divide in this manner. At the beginning of the May harvest, two of the farmers go through the fields and mark out the cott grass from the known grounds, then two other farmers follow, and divide it into so many proportional parts as there are freeholders.[1]

Unfortunately the accompanying map is missing. It is thought the fields lay mostly to the north of the main road, with the roads to Laughton and Foxton meeting at the Green forming the boundaries separating the three fields. Work is underway to try to match the names listed in the survey to present day field names.

By the 18th century, demands on farming nationally were changing. The population was increasing and there was need for more food. Wealthy farmers and graziers felt they could not meet the demand when their lands were divided into strips dispersed throughout the village. This led to the Enclosure Acts whereby, rather than collective ownership, land became the property of a few, thus creating a landless peasantry.

Lubenham parish was finally enclosed by an Act of 1766. There had been an earlier movement in 1600 when the Lord of the Manor, Sir Basil Brooke, agreed on enclosure with 17 of his tenants in order to alleviate his serious financial problems. This resulted in an unusually large number of freeholders with small estates in the village.

Sir Basil was summoned before Star Chamber to explain his actions. He

> **Star Chamber**, so called because its ceiling was decorated with stars, was an English court of law in 15th–17th centuries, made up of privy councillors and common law judges, established to ensure fair enforcement of law against prominent people who might otherwise use their power to influence the ordinary courts. It was abolished in 1641.

59

said his motive was poverty, claiming that the income from the manor and rents from 13 farms was insufficient to maintain his many children and the burdensome offices he undertook![2]

The total area concerned in the Enclosure Award of 1766 was around 1233 acres of which the largest allotment was granted to John Wright, Lord of the Manor. These changes meant the traditional work of the poor (weeding, threshing and so on) all but disappeared and many workers had to rely on the charity of the parish. According to Parish Records of 1784 to 1792, 54 people in Lubenham were buried as paupers. This may be due in part to changes in agriculture.

Fifteen years after enclosure, 42% of the parish was owner-occupied and in the following years there was extensive conversion to pastureland. By the 1831 census, 71 men out of the 148 over the age of 20 were still employed in agriculture, 17 as farmers and 54 as labourers.

From the 19th to the mid 20th century small to medium sized family farms predominated, mainly mixed with arable, sheep and cattle. Farms in the village, including Adams, the White House and Paget Arms, had a small paddock, outbuildings for cows and pigs, stables, and storage barns, with the remaining land usually situated elsewhere in the parish. Milk was sold locally or sent in churns to dairies in Market

Above: Teatime in the Hayfield, 1903: Mr Vendy, Ezra Spriggs, Mr Goode, Edward Carter, E. Davis, J. Goode, F. Taylor.

Earning a Living

View across Welland Valley.

Harborough and North Kilworth. Cattle were walked from nearby markets or brought by rail from as far as Wales and Ireland to be fattened on the rich pastures of the Welland Valley. In autumn animals were sent for slaughter to cities such as London and Birmingham.

Manor Farm was somewhat different from other family run businesses. For much of the 20th century it was in the tenancy of the Ashton family and before World War II was part of a large enterprise extending over 3,000 acres. The *History of the County of Leicester*[3] describes the property as 'one of Leicestershire's famous grazing farms'.

Major changes took place during World War II. A large parcel of land on an area known as Foxton Moor was taken for the construction of an airfield with substantial buildings demolished and many ridge and furrow fields levelled. Elsewhere, the Ministry of Agriculture ordered that every suitable field should be ploughed to grow vital food crops such as wheat, oats and potatoes. After the

Edward Carter washing sheep at the Washpit (in Washpit Lane, off Westgate Lane) in 1922. The river Welland was damned, diverting water into a channel. Now derelict, sections of the brickwork can still be seen.

61

war much of this land reverted to grazing but subsequent changes in agricultural practice and the introduction of large machinery has again led to a prevalence of arable farming in the area. In the 1950s there were 15 small to medium sized family farms in the parish. Fifty years later, with one exception, these had disappeared as the land was sold or rented out to farmers from elsewhere, part of the national trend towards larger, more cost effective units.

Combining in the 1970s.

Trades and businesses

Throughout the centuries the main preoccupation in Lubenham was to provide enough food for the village population. The area would have been largely self-sufficient with specialist tradesmen, people like the charcoal burner, cooper, potter, brick maker, wheelwright, weaver, miller, cordwainer and blacksmith. Later, especially from Stuart times onwards, travelling salesmen would visit with items often not available locally such as tools, salt, salted fish or luxury goods like lace, ribbons and combs.

It is interesting to note some of the occupations listed in the Parish Register for 1719 – miller, chandler (dealer in household items such as oil), mercer (cloth dealer), cordwainer (shoe maker), brick maker, examiner of excise (a tax man) and flax dressers.

Amongst those who died in 1754 were a comber (person who combs wool or cloth), horse breaker, wadman (wad is material to keep powder or shot in a gun barrel), ragman, bricklayer, rat catcher, maltster, school master and excise man as well as numerous weavers and yeomen.

The 19th century was period of great change. By extracting details from directories and gazetteers published by William White, Kelly, Wright and others between the 1820s and 1940s, it is possible to get a snapshot of the businesses that existed in Lubenham. They fall into three main groups; those associated with food (grocers, bakers, etc.), trades and craftsmen (tailors, shoe makers, etc.) and other miscellaneous occupations.

1. Food and drink

Most villagers would have grown their own vegetables in gardens or allotments. The Village Green (more correctly Lubenham Green Gardens) was formerly allotments and the book of Rules and Regulations drawn up in 1868 is still in force today. However, there was a need for other provisions, most notably bread, milk and meat.

Earning a Living

Fred Pateman and William Tilley delivering bread in School Lane in the 1930s.

Until the windmill on Mill Hill burnt down around 1886/7 corn was ground into flour locally and used by bakers in the village. The Old Bake House on The Green shows the door on the upper level where sacks were hauled up and the bread oven is *in situ* in the room below. Three families of bakers, Knight, Tilley and Pateman, prevail from the early 1800s onwards and the firm of Tilley & Pateman was still working from the Old Bake House when it finally closed in 1940s.

One of the earliest directories, that of Pigot & Co in 1822, lists two butchers, John Coleman and John Ellson. They carried on trading until the 1880s when

The village allotments are still subject to the regulations drawn up in 1868.

Shops in Lubenham

Miller's shop, Main Street (opposite the *Coach and Horses*, now a private house): Miss Lambert in the doorway of Miller's Shop and Post Office, early 1900s.

Collins shop (The Drapers House) on Main Street, next to the Coach & Horses.

The Drapers House in 2012: an antique shop but up for sale – ready for its next reincarnation?

Earning a Living

> **Gilson Pick** was born in Lincolnshire in 1877 and fought in the Boer War. He and his family moved to Lubenham and in the 1911 Census was listed as a butcher, and later as a farmer and grazier. He is still remembered by some in the village as 'a bit of a character'. A good horseman, notably cautious with his money, he was easily recognisable by his gloved hand, the result of an injury sustained in the 1930s working the sausage machine. He would always carry his delivery basket over this arm, leaving his good hand free to do the work. He died in 1964 aged 87.

Thomas Hart and Benjamin Measures took over, to be followed by Arthur Rawson. By World War I the names George Stafford and Gilson Pick appear, Stafford occupying the shop at Rose Cottage on the corner of Main Street and The Green whilst Pick owned Western Villa in Westgate Lane where there was also a slaughterhouse. As a farmer and grazier, Pick sold his home-produced meat in his shop on Main Street and neighbouring villages. Both businesses closed in the 1960s.

George Burditt Jnr delivering milk from White House Farm on Main Street in the 1950s.

Apart from a few years around 1900 when the name Putterill appears, no dairymen are shown in any of the directories or gazetteers, presumably because milk was supplied directly from farms. The Tithe Register of 1845, for example, lists William Hart as a grazier and dairyman, and even 100 years later milk was still delivered in the village by families such as the Burditts of White House Farm. Their round was taken over by Jack Barwick who, like William Hart, owned a dairy behind Eden House. The round ceased in 1962–3.

One of the most iconic aspects of rural life is the village shop. Until the 1980s Lubenham had two such shops selling groceries, confectionary, newspapers, wines and spirits and even knitting wool and firewood. They were situated on either side of the Main Road although in 19th century two other shops were also listed. Many

> I remember Fred Piper as quite a big man, sweeping outside his shop every morning as we went to school. He was the most jovial shopkeeper you could imagine. Wearing his big white apron he would weigh out such things as sugar and currants in little blue bags and slice and weigh butter and lard. The shop also had a haberdashery department and sold everything we needed for making and mending clothes.
>
> *Fred Piper as remembered by Margaret Bale (née Woolmer)*

of the shop proprietors were women: Ann Allen in 1820s and later Eileen Collins, Elizabeth Line, Jemima Miller and Ethel Simmons (née Haynes). The last shop, Lubenham News, closed in April 2002.

One name remembered with affection is that of Fred Piper, who ran the shop next to the pub from just after World War I until he retired in the 1950s.

One of the earliest references to the Post Office was in *White's Directory and Gazetteer* of 1846 which says 'it was at Jno Smalley's which received letters from Welford daily'. By the 1860s the post office was situated in one of the shops on Main Street, the name of the post master or mistress being synonymous with that of the shop keeper – Joseph Collins, Edwin and Jemima Miller, Harold Simmons, and so on. In 1863 letters were sent from Rugby at 7.00am and despatched at 7.10pm. A few years later letters were received from Market Harborough at 6.35am and sent at 6.20pm. It is interesting to note the very precise times given! The village post office, which by this time was situated at the garage on Main Street, finally closed in 2006.

2. Trades and craftsmen

At the beginning of the 19th century there were several craftsmen in Lubenham but over the next 100 years these trades disappeared. It is easy to speculate that this was the result of the growing importance of Market Harborough where directories list numerous entries for builders and associated trades as well as specialist shops such as drapers, ironmongers, tailors and booksellers. Harborough was also the centre for professional services – banks, solicitors, insurance agents, doctors and chemists.

Throughout the Victorian period there were dressmakers and tailors such as George Hopkins, Henry Garlick, Thomas Norman and Fred Wilford in the village. Boot and shoe makers and repairers were also common with at least four in the 1820s, names like Goode, Cockerill, Eldridge and Tomkins. However, these occupations had all vanished by the early 20th century.

Building trades suffered a similar fate. Early names such as Platt and Pickering and carpenters Putt, Spriggs and Martin are not listed after 1880, although one carpenter, Edward Carter, did return and worked until the 1930s. In contrast, builders, electricians, plumbers, roofers and other related services are the most common businesses in the village today, often sole traders or employing a few people.

3. Other businesses

Coal merchants: John Tebbutt was listed as a coal merchant in *White's Directory* of 1846 at a time when coal was carried by canal to Lubenham wharf. The opening of the railway station in 1869 meant that coal could be brought in by rail and by the late 1880s there were three dealers in the village. In the 1920s J. Millington started a coal merchants business on Main Street on a site which was later converted into a garage and petrol station.

Timber merchants: Around 1904 John Wiggington established a timber firm at what is now Piper's Piece, later moving the business to The Limes near Washpit Lane.

Earning a Living

Here he used a steam-driven saw to cut locally obtained timber.

Blacksmiths: Lubenham was a centre for horses and farming and the blacksmith not only shod horses but made and repaired tools and other farm implements. The first name to appear in the directories was Thomas Perkins in 1822 followed by John Burditt who had a forge on Main Street opposite Westgate Lane. By 1880 there were two, John Checkley from *The Coach and Horses* and Jabez Payne, who came to Lubenham from Sharnbrook in Bedfordshire in 1878. He set up business in a house near the railway station which is believed to be that opposite what is now Paget Road, before moving to a site in Rushes Lane. Jabez and later his two sons carried on the business until it was taken over by Monty Connell in the 1950s. The forge closed in the 1980s. There was another blacksmith's shop run by Alfred Newman at Rose Cottage from around 1900 to 1930.

Clockmakers: For several years George Rimmington and son worked as specialist clock and watchmakers in the village. An example of their work is found on Clock Cottage to the rear of Gore Lodge.

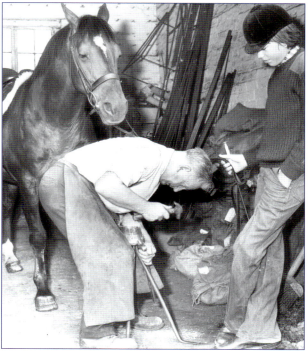

Top: Blacksmith Jabez Payne and wife, Lettice. In the 1950s their business was taken on by Monty Connell, **pictured right** at work in August 1976. Looking on is rider Tom Walker of Laughton. Connell's name lives on in Connell Close.

Public Houses:[4] *The Coach and Horses*, previously *The White Swan*, dates from at least 1700 according to a brick on the front of the building, although it is almost certainly much older than that. A classic coaching inn with stables and blacksmith's shop to the rear, it would have been an important stop on the turnpike road from Harborough to Coventry. The other public house, built in the 19th century, was the *Paget Arms*, formerly the *Red Cow*. It closed in 1961 and is now a private house.

Other businesses have come and gone during the last century. Local people were employed as drivers and office staff by St Mary's Transport when their general and livestock lorries were based in School Lane for around 30 years after World War II. A lingerie factory in Rushes Lane, occupying stables belonging to The Tower House, employed up to 60 people, mainly women. It was a big loss of employment when it was forced to close soon after a disastrous fire in April 2001.

Above: The Paget Arms in the early 1900s. **Below:** Fire destroys the lingerie factory in Rushes Lane in 2001 – a major employer in the village.

Earning a Living

The Perkins' factories

The name Joshua Perkins dominated employment in Lubenham for over half a century and yet the early history of the factories is somewhat obscure. Recent research[5] shows a family connection dating back to the 1760s when Thomas, a weaver, settled in the village and later worked with his son, also Thomas (b. 1767) in their own weaving shed. It appears that Thomas Jnr continued to run this as a cottage indus-

Above: Victoria Mills in School Lane, c. 1900. **Below:** School Lane in 1904, showing the west side of Victoria Mills and workers' cottages.

69

LOT 5.

(Coloured Green on Plan).

THE SUBSTANTIAL MODERN

FACTORY PREMISES

KNOWN AS

"Victoria Mills," Lubenham

together with

Six Cottages, Gardens and Paddock

numbered part Nos. 233, and 218 and No. 232 on plan, area about

1a. 1r. 34p.

The Property

Is situate on the East side of and with a frontage 402 feet or thereabouts to School Lane, ample yard space has been allowed to avoid any congestion and the land to the south provides exceptional opportunities for future extensions.

The Principal Building

Is substantially built of brick with slated roof and blue brick floor. It is well lighted and ventilated and comprises Entrance Lobby 22ft. 6in. by 8ft. and to the right, Warehouse and Office 22ft. 6in. by 32ft. and immediately over there is a Stock Room 40ft. by 22ft. 6in The remainder of the accommodation is entirely on the ground floor and comprises

The Main Shed, 62ft. 6ins. by 100ft.

communicating with Engine House 33ft. by 18ft. 6in., Boiler House 22ft. 6in. by 16ft. (with "Robin Hood" Boiler) by *Messrs. Ashwell & Nesbitt, Ltd.,* Lavatory 13ft. by 15ft. 6in., Plant House, 8ft. by 6ft. (with electric light plant, consisting of 42 brake H.P. Crossley Gas Engine "u" type, Dynamo by *B.T.H., Rugby,* 15 K.W.), Lighting Shed (corrugated roof) 25ft. by 7ft., Gas House 26ft. by 19ft., Glass Shed 46ft. by 9ft. and Stock Room East 18ft. 6in. by 42ft. making a total

Floor Space 11,129 Square Feet

Electric Light, Central Heating, Company's Gas and Water, Telephone, Modern Drainage, together with the adjoining brick-built and slated

Eight Cottages with Gardens

Let as Six, each containing Sitting Room, Kitchen, 2 Bedrooms and the usual out offices, Let to Messrs. Downes, Ashton, Peake, Dunkley, Howard and Dunkley, on weekly tenancies at gross rentals amounting to £50 14s. 0d. per annum, and

Paddock

Let to Mr. J. T. Smith on a yearly tenancy, at rental of £4 per annum.

The Sale of this Lot affords an unique opportunity to acquire a substantial modern factory close to the Town of Market Harborough, with its excellent Railway facilities, and within five minutes walk of Lubenham Railway Station (Rugby to Peterborough branch). The Property is in the market solely on account of Messrs. Joshua Perkins & Son (1909) Ltd. having decided to concentrate their business at Coventry.

The sales catalogue for Victoria Mills, 1923.

try using home workers until the 1840s. However, there is some evidence that as early as the mid-1830s he had a factory in Husbands Bosworth which employed 20 men making/shaping hats using the silk plush made in Lubenham. Thomas Perkins was an enterprising man, not only recorded as a manufacturer but listed in trade directories of the 1820s onwards as shopkeeper, beer retailer, blacksmith, miller and corn merchant. He married twice and had 12 children. Of the ten who survived, several emigrated to America. The three who remained in the village were Sarah, who ran the grocer's shop and post office; Ann, who married Daniel Tilley the baker; and Joshua.

Joshua appears to have taken over from his father in the mid 1840s and by the 1843 edition of *Whites* he was listed as a silk plush manufacturer, the same directory noting that 'some of the inhabitants are employed in making silk plush for hats'. Where this work took place or how many people were involved is unknown but by 1850, at the age of 33, Joshua had amassed enough money to build The Laurels on Main Street at a cost of £20,000, the equivalent of more than £1.5m in 2010.

In Whites Directory and Gazetteer of 1863 Joshua Perkins is no longer listed as a maker of silk plush but as a manufacturer of ketchup and pickles, carriage and livery lace. The ketchup and pickles were made in a factory in Rushes Lane, later the site of a garage. Carriage and livery lace trimmings were sold to the principal railway companies and coach builders both here and abroad. According to an 1896 article in the journal *Coventry Up-to-Date*, 'Messrs Perkins had long been established in the markets of the world as a leading firm in this branch of the textile industry, making products of the highest quality in a variety of materials and design.'

Victoria Mills stood in School Lane on a site now occupied by housing. Photographs show this to be a large, imposing structure but the style of architecture indicates that it would not have been built before the early 1840s. The design and layout of the factory are recorded in detail in the 1923 Sale Catalogue, although the date when the machinery was installed is not known. In 1864 Perkins opened a factory in Coventry which was later run by his sons Joshua, Joseph Smith and William. A new factory, Britannia Mills, was erected on Payne's Lane Coventry in 1878 and the description of that building is remarkably similar to Victoria Mills, Lubenham. It is quite possible that both premises were constructed around the same time.

It is hard to imagine what it would have been like working in a large, noisy factory such as Victoria Mills. How many people were actually employed is uncertain, the trades directories and *History of the County of Leicester*[3] referring to 'many' or 'a substantial number', but it is known that around 200 were associated with the Coventry factory.

Victoria Mills closed and was sold along with several other properties in 1923 when Perkins transferred all their business to the Coventry site which itself closed in 1930s. The demand for their products had gone and with it an important part of Lubenham's history.

71

References

[1] Bermingham. *A Book of References to the several lands including map of Lubenham, belonging to Samuel Wright*, 1734

[2] Nichols, John. *The History and Antiquities of the County of Leicester*, volume 11, part 11, 1798.

[3] *History of the County of Leicestershire*, volume 5, Gartree Hundred, 1964.

[4] See Chapter 9, *Time off*.

[5] Perkins, Lawrence and Christine. Private correspondence.

― *Village Characters* ―

Fred Pateman chatting to Mrs Tilley, c. 1880

7. Village characters

Every village needs its 'characters', individuals who for whatever reason – famous or infamous, rich, idiosyncratic – stand out from the crowd, but it is the ordinary men and women, going about their daily lives, who form the backbone and strength of the community.

Bernard Patrick, who can trace his family back to the 1600s in Lubenham.

The Patrick family can trace their ancestry in Lubenham to the 1600s. The Burditts, Tilleys and several others have been associated with the village since the 1700s. The Sprigg family goes back even further in the records. The earliest mention was in 1327 when Robert, Edward and Thomas Sprigg appear in the Gartree Subsidy Roll as freeholders. More than 150 years later a member of the same family won distinction at the Battle of Bosworth Field and in 1645 yet another was thought to be chaplain to Sir Thomas Fairfax at the Battle of Naseby. The last surviving member of the family in Lubenham died in 1983.

Other names which have appeared over the decades in Church records, trade directories, and school accounts include Carter, Cockerill, Goode, Pateman, Miller, Collins, Payne, Coleman, Eldridge, Iliffe and Platt. Many of these were farm workers, labourers or those associated with various trades and businesses in the village.

One such family was the Perkins[1]. Although no longer linked to Lubenham, they influenced village life for over a century as shopkeepers, beer retailers, blacksmiths and most notably as factory owners, making silk plush, carriage and livery trim-

73

mings and ketchup and pickles. Joshua Perkins died in January 1896 leaving an estate valued at £26,285.10s, equivalent to £2,370,000 in 2010.

But what of Lubenham's many 'characters'? One name which immediately springs to mind is **Jack 'Cherry' Angell**. Famed for his eccentricities and penchant for the cherry red colour which he used for his hunting coat and Phaeton carriage, Angell has left a unique legacy in Lubenham. Born Benedict John Angell Brown in 1828 into a fabulously wealthy London family, he later dropped the name Brown, preferring instead his great grandmother's name of Angell. It was his love of hunting and racing which brought him to the village.

The sons of Joshua Perkins.

He purchased The Cottage, now The Tower House, gradually enlarging the house and then the estate to include Gore Lodge, The Dower House and adjacent Stud Groom's Cottage, Adam's Farm, The Coach and Horses pub and over 200 acres of land. He built stables to accommodate his horses, which included Grand National winner *Alcibiade*, and was instrumental in establishing a four-mile steeplechase in Lubenham which later became the centrepiece of the Cheltenham Festival.[2] Sadly this unconventional yet influential man died childless in 1874 aged only 46. The estate was sold but his legacy lives on.

Another character who has left an indelible mark on the village is **Henry Everard Bullivant**, rector of Lubenham for 52 years from 1842 to 1894. Many of the institutions and organisations still around today owe their existence to his hard work. His tireless campaigning led to the opening of the railway station 19 years after the line itself. He was instrumental in building the village school, raising money and organising the committee of which he was both chairman and secretary. Similarly he was responsible for co–ordinating the management of Lubenham Green Gardens and drawing up a constitution and book of rules, both of

Photograph believed to be of Jack 'Cherry' Angell.

Village Characters

which still govern the running of the allotments and Village Green today. Despite all his other commitments, Henry Everard Bullivant devoted his life to the church serving the spiritual needs of the village. He even donated his own house on The Green, which was used as a rectory until its sale in the 1980s. A commemorative plaque can be found in the parish church.

Born in 1581, **David Papillon** came from an influential French Huguenot family. At the age of seven David, his mother and sisters were sent to England to avoid the continuing persecution of the Huguenots in France. Unfortunately, his mother died in a shipwreck on the journey and the Papillon children were brought up by family and friends. David was apprenticed to a Master Jeweller but at the age of 23 he decided to follow a career in military engineering. He became a noted expert, writing many treatises and drawing up the plans for the fortification of Northampton amongst other places. In 1609, a year after his father's death, David and his brothers-in-law began trading in precious stones. He was so successful that he was commissioned by Charles I to oversee the redemption of the Crown Jewels which had been pawned in Holland. Here was a very important, influential and wealthy man who chose to build his house, Papillon Hall, in Lubenham.[3]

Above: David Papillon 1581–1658. **Below:** the family crest with its motto Ditat servata fides – 'Keeping faith enriches'. It certainly did in his case.

Captain Frank Bellville, whose family fortune came from the manufacture of Robinson's Barley Water, was given Papillon Hall by his mother in 1903 and immediately commissioned Sir Edwin Lutyens to redesign the house and gardens. Frank Bellville died in July 1937, aged 67. He had three wives, six children and three stepchildren. Rupert, his eldest son and heir, was reputedly the first Englishman to become a bullfighter in Spain, a country he loved so much that he painted the entrance pillars to Papillon Hall in the Spanish national colours of red and yellow! A dashing old Etonian, Rupert was a test pilot during World War II, having previously flown in Franco's air force at the start of the Spanish Civil War. He was taken prisoner in Spain but escaped being shot after vehemently protesting that he was English and was eventually rescued by a British gunboat. Rupert married an American and his son Hercules 'Herky' Bellville became a noted film producer.

Amongst the many owners and tenants of the Old Hall, formerly Baud's Manor, there are two of particular interest. **Sir Ranulph Crewe** (1558 to 1646) owned the Hall but was an absentee landlord. Described as 'a man of the people' he was an important legal figure, MP, Speaker and Lord Chief Justice who was ignominiously removed from his post and sent to The Tower by King James I for refusing to subscribe to a legal document on forced loans and objecting to an increase in taxation. Ironically, Crewe was Lord of the Manor when James' son Charles I stayed at the Old Hall before the Battle of Naseby with the then tenant Mr Collins.

Dr Samuel Wright was a noted 18th century theologian and philanthropist from Stoke Newington in London. He left considerable sums of money to charities, schools, hospitals and prison and welfare reform as well as to individuals, including the poor and others in Lubenham. A copy of his will can be found in Nichols' *History and Antiquities of the County of Leicester.*[2]

Reginald 'Reggie' Paget was born into a wealthy Leicestershire landowning family in 1908. He lived for several years at Lubenham Lodge, inheriting the title of Lord of the Manor from his father. Reggie was a brilliant barrister, author and Labour MP for Northampton for nearly 30 years. He was made a life peer in 1975. A man of principle, he worked at a war crimes tribunal in 1949, having 'stuck his

At one time the Paget family could ride from Melton Mowbray to Northampton only leaving their own land for two fields.

As remembered by John Dyke in conversation with Lord Reginald Paget.

Right:
Lord Paget in 1979

neck out' to defend the German Field Marshall Erich von Manstein, free of charge. However, he will be remembered, rather affectionately, for his eccentricities and love of hunting. Harold Macmillan once said 'he certainly deserves to be remembered as more than just another of the great eccentrics … English political life will be poorer and neither the Tories nor the foxes much happier'!

Thorpe Lubenham Hall has been the home of several wealthy, influential families.[3] **Gordon Cunard**, a member of the shipping dynasty, lived in the house at the end of the 19th century, buying the freehold in 1912. Eight years later the Hall was purchased by **Sir Harold Wernher**. He had inherited a vast fortune from his father's gold and diamond mining interests in Southern Africa. His wife, **Lady Zia**, was a member of the Russian royal family and their marriage in 1917 caused a sensation at the time. Dividing their schedule between London, Scotland and Thorpe Lubenham, the Wernhers set about improving the Hall, building an extension, covered tennis courts, polo field and golf course. They lived here in considerable style, employing around 28 staff on the estate.

Village Characters

The Rev. Moffat Peake accompanies HM Queen Elizabeth to All Saints Church. Also shown are HRH Prince Philip, Prince Charles, Princess Anne, Capt. Phillips, Mrs Georgina Phillips (née Wernher) and their children.

A keen huntsman, Sir Harold began breeding and owing racehorses, the most famous of which was the legendary *Brown Jack*, winner of the Alexander Stakes at Ascot an incredible six years in succession. Members of the Royal Family were frequent visitors to the house, especially during the 1950s when the Queen and Prince Philip were guests of daughter Georgina Wernher and her husband Colonel Philips.

The house was purchased in 1966 by (Geoffrey) Lionel Berry, 2nd Viscount Kemsley, the son of James Berry, a prominent newspaper baron and owner of *The Sunday Times* and *Daily Sketch*. Berry served in the Grenadier Guards during the Second World War before being elected unopposed as MP for Buckingham in 1943, losing his seat to Labour in the 1945 General Election. He was managing editor of the *Daily Sketch* and deputy chairman of Kemsley Newspapers Ltd which controlled not only *The Sunday Times* but also several daily and evening provincial newspapers. By the time he succeeded his father to the title in 1968, the newspaper business had been sold to the Thomson Group.

He married Helene, daughter of the 11th Marquis of Tweeddale in 1933 and

---

In World War II, General Sir Harold Wernher played a key role as co-ordinator between the War Office and various ministries concerned with the building and deployment of the Mulberry Harbours used on D-Day.

Rear-Admiral Hickling in a lecture given in March 1945 said Sir Harold 'carried out a very difficult job in a most able fashion. Above all he kept the peace between the more irascible members and reconciled the conflicting interests and priorities.'

they had four daughters. Viscount Kemsley died in 1999 aged 89. The house was sold in 1985 to Sir Bruce and Lady Caroline MacPhail, who have continued the close relationship with the village and All Saints Church.

References

[1] See Chapter 6, *Earning a living*.
[2] See Chapter 10, *Horses and hunting*.
[3] See Chapter 5, *Mansions and cottages*
[4] Nichols, John. *The History and Antiquities of the County of Leicester*, volume 2, part 2, 1798.

War & Remembrance

8. War and remembrance

The War Memorial, a simple stone monument, stands as a tribute to the men from Lubenham who died in the First and Second World Wars.

The War Memorial on its original site c. 1930. Note the Women's Unionist Hall (now the Village Hall) in the background.

Despite its proximity to the busy main road, it is a place of peace and tranquillity, surrounded by trees and bushes and fronted by a well tended lawn. Situated on the site of the former village pond, the Memorial was moved here in 1949 from its original position on Main Street opposite Westgate Lane. A committee of volunteers from the village is responsible for the upkeep of the Memorial and the surrounding gardens. A Service of Remembrance is held every year on Armistice Day when the names of all those who died are read out.

A stained glass window in All Saints Church was installed in 1947 in memory of Captain George (Alex) Wernher of Thorpe Lubenham Hall who was killed in action in North Africa in 1942 (see page 30).

The parish was a hive of activity during World War II. The airfield was built in 1942–3 on prime agricultural land. It housed an Oper-

The dedication of the memorial.

ational Training Unit (OTU) from June 1943, flying mainly Wellington bombers. During the next two years the OTU trained nearly 3,000 personnel – pilots, navigators, wireless operators, bomb aimers and air gunners. Sixty-one men lost their lives during exercises.

The airfield was used by the RAF until April 1947 when the residential quarters were taken over by the Ministry of Housing to house displaced persons, mainly Polish. The Camp, as it became known locally, had its own church, cinema and shop, whilst most of the children attended St Joseph's Roman Catholic School in Harborough. Numbers dwindled and by the late 1950s the land was returned to agriculture and the huts demolished or used as farm buildings.

The former runways and hangers were used as a vehicle depot for the Royal Army Ordnance Corps until 1959–60 and the rest of the site gradually reverted to farming. HMP Gartree and associated housing were opened in 1966.

Papillon Hall, known locally as Pamp's Hall, was requisitioned to house military personnel including the Seaforth Highlanders and later members of the American 319 Glider Field Artillery (82nd Airborne Division), many of whom saw action on D-Day. The Laurels on Main Street was used as a military hospital.

Don Johnson who helped his father collect pig swill from the RAF camp and Pamp Hall's recalls:

Americans at Papillon Hall.

War & Remembrance

Above: Members of the Home Guard in Lubenham, 1944. **Below:** A decaying Nissen hut on the old airfield site. **Bottom right:** There's much more to the Battlefield Headquarters on the old airfield than meets the eye. It is of a relatively rare type, with five underground rooms, including an office and a private branch exchange (PBX) with only an observation cupola or dome visible above ground. BHQs were intended only for use when an airfield was under attack.

The Americans were a smiling, fun-loving people who were generous and friendly, especially to a small boy such as me. I received many unasked for luxuries – chocolates, sweets, cheese, gum, Swiss roll and oranges. It was a sad day when the 82nd Glider Unit marched from Pamp's Hall to Market Harborough en route south. We were waving goodbye to people who were open and friendly (especially if you had a sister!) who had brought life into Lubenham such as we had never seen before.

The story of the Land Army Hostel and the girls who lived there is told in Pat Fox's book *Bless 'Em All*.[1] The purpose-

81

Lubenham Village History

NORTH MIDLAND CIVIL DEFENCE REGION

COMBINED MILITARY AND CIVIL DEFENCE SCHEME FOR LUBENHAM.

Signed _____ (Military Commander)

Signed _____ (Chairman)

Countersigned _____

Explanatory Note:—This outline of a Defence Scheme is arranged in seven parts, under the seven headings given on Page 26 (Appendix B) of the "Consolidated Instructions to Invasion Committees." The figures entered in brackets are references to the relevant paragraphs of the Consolidated Instructions.

The outline is intended primarily for the use of Invasion Committees in those villages, etc., where there is no organisation of the Local Authority, complete with clerical staff and equipment, to be put at the Committee's disposal. At such places, the clerical work of drafting the scheme may be lightened by using as a draft the outline itself, and by entering local particulars under each heading, duly introducing additional sheets when necessary.

Above and opposite: Combined Military and Civil Defence Scheme for Lubenham, and the Invasion Committee.

Right: the menu for the Home Guard Stand Down Supper, December 20th 1944.

Menu

CREAM VEGETABLE SOUP.

———

ROAST CHICKEN and SAUSAGE.

MIXED SALAD.

MAYONAISE.

———

TRIFLES.   ∴   PASTRIES.

CHEESE and CELERY.

COFFEE.

LUBENHAM — COMBINED CIVIL AND MILITARY DEFENCE SCHEME

PART 1.—THE INVASION COMMITTEE (C.I.3)

List of names, addresses and telephone numbers of (a) members of the Committee, and (b) persons on the additional panel of other local officials, etc., who may be consulted or co-opted for advice and help when necessary.

(a) Members of the Committee.

Appointment or Service represented.	Name.	Address.	Tel. No.
Chairman	Geo Burditt	White House Lubenham	
Military			
Police	Supt Kelly	Mkt Harboro	2251
A.R.P.	Mr J Carter	4 Foxton Rd Lubenham	022
N.F.S.	F Piper	Lubenham	
Food	Mr J Carter	4 Foxton Rd Lubenham	2392
Highways	L.C.C.		Kibworth 86
Women's Services	Mrs R Barr	Lubenham	2319
Water		154 Coventry Rd	2273

(b) Members of the Additional Panel.

Emplt. Ex. Mngr.	Brookes	31 Coventry Rd Mkt Harb	2167
Relieving Officer	Mr Ford Jun	Victoria Avenue Mkt Harboro	2194
Billeting Officer	Mr P Miller	Coach & Horses Lubenham	
Asstce. Brd. Offr.	Mr Yoxham	Vic. Avenue Mkt Harboro	
Postmaster	H Simons		022
Information Offr.	Mr F Piper	Main St Lubenham	
Gas Officer	Mr Harris	Mkt Harboro U.D.C.	2133
Electricity Offr.		Kettering U.D.C.	2171

Note.—On (a) entries : The Deputy Chairman should be indicated by an asterisk, or his name should be inserted separately, whichever is appropriate.

Note.—On (b) entries : There may be no representative in the village, but it may be useful to record the particulars of the nearest of such officers who might have to be consulted.

built hostel, situated on the corner of Foxton Road and The Green, comprised a brick built ablution block, a large wooden dormitory, dining room and kitchen and separate quarters for the wardens. The girls were allocated to farms throughout the Welland Valley. The work was long, hard and often dangerous but Pat tells of the camaraderie and life-long friendships that developed.

Life for ordinary villagers became more regulated. A local Home Guard group was formed and a Civil Defence Scheme established, the latter responsible for practical arrangements such as identifying buildings suitable for housing in an emergency, maintaining a reserve food store and issuing gas masks. In addition, eight ARP (Air Raid Precaution) wardens, 72 Fire Guards (24 parties of three) and 18 First Aid personnel were appointed. Lubenham was ready to fight its war!

Reference
[1] Fox, Pat. *Bless 'Em All!* Market Harborough Historical Society, 2010.

The Leicestershire Yeomanry

The Leicestershire Yeomanry passing Lubenham Station and stationmaster's house in 1923, taken from Railway Bridge across the main road.

The Yeomanry was raised in 1794 in response to government demands for the formation of a volunteer corps to counteract the threat of a French invasion. In 1900 two companies (the 7th and 65th) saw service in the South Africa Wars. At the outbreak of war in 1914 the regiment was mobilised and saw action at Ypres in 1914 and again in 1915 where at the Battle of Frezenberg a squadron held the line for the entire brigade. After the First World War the regiment was reformed in the Territorial Army, continuing as part of the Cavalry Corps until the Second World War when it converted to a field artillery role. The Leicestershire Yeomanry camped regulary at Papillon Hall Farm and attended church parades at All Saints Church.

A Leicestershire Yeomanry Camp in Lubenham, 1927.

9. Time off: Leisure and recreation

The Village Hall

The original wooden hall was formally opened in June 1927 by Lord Castlesteward who thought 'it was one of the most magnificent huts of its kind in the county' and predicted that 'this building will be the centre of life in Lubenham'. Consisting of a large room 57 x 23 feet plus a kitchen and cloakrooms, it was constructed on land given by the Paget family. Money for the building was collected in the village with the balance being given by Lady Zia Wernher of Thorpe Lubenham on condition that it was called the Women's Unionist Hall. It became known as the Village Hall in 1976.

The building came to life during World War II when it was the venue for regular dances. As one villager recalled:

The hut, heated by coke-filled stoves, was filled to overcapacity and with everyone exuding pent-up energy and gyrating to the music it was not difficult to understand why it was called 'The Sweat Box'.

By 1992, despite an on-going maintenance programme, the Hall had fallen into disrepair and a grant was obtained to build a new frontage which included an entrance hall, kitchen, store rooms and toilets. In 2004 the old wooden structure was demolished completely and replaced by the present enlarged brick building, paid for by local grants and awards as well as extensive fund-raising in the village. A further extension was added in 2007, funded by an anonymous benefactor, and plans to en-

Lubenham Village History

Above: The original wooden village hall shortly before it was demolished.
Below: The 2004 improvements.

large and refurbish the kitchen and toilets are in the pipeline.

As predicted at the opening ceremony in 1927, the Village Hall is an important centre of village life, being used by many local groups including the Playgroup, Brownies, Short Mat Bowls Club, Welcome Club, Heritage Group, whist

Left: Short mat bowls.

Time Off

drives, Art Club and Drama Group as well as for other fundraising and charity events.

It is an attractive venue with good facilities and both rooms, the Main Hall with a seating capacity of over 100, and the smaller Onyx Room are heavily booked.

The Village Green

> 'a certain piece of ground lying near or within the town of Lubenham called The Green or Township, which piece of ground is left out for the use of the Inhabitants of Lubenham aforesaid'
>
> **Enclosure Act 1767**

The Green is a large, attractive area with trees and surrounded by a hedge which, like the Playing Fields and Village Hall is run by Trustees on behalf of the village. However, this is not a traditional Village Green but Green Gardens used as allotments from the time of the Enclosures until the 1980s when growing your own food fell out of fashion and the area was put down to grass.

Under the Enclosure Act of 1767 around four and a quarter acres in the village were not enclosed and left for use by the inhabitants, mainly as allotments.

However, in 1857 several occupants challenged the practice of the Lord of the Manor, Thomas Paget, to charge rent and two, Thomas Cotton and William Goode, were sued for refusing to pay. The matter was settled out of court, the consequences of which still govern the management of The Green today. Paget agreed that the gardens should be the responsibility of Trustees, all of whom he nominated. The Trustees and their heirs would let the plots to Lubenham inhabitants, charging rent which would then be used for the upkeep of the land. *The Constitution and Rules*

87

& Regulations, formally adopted in April 1868, specified how the area was to be managed. For example:
- The general size of the garden shall be about 200 square yards.
- No building, shed or pigsty shall be erected.
- No dunghill or manure heap allowed to accumulate so as to become a nuisance.
- All resident householders are eligible as garden occupiers.
- Every occupier shall pay 1 shilling annually towards the necessary current expenses.

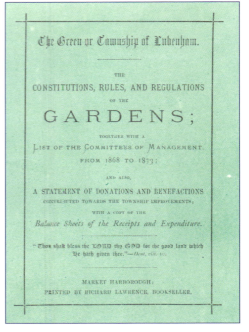

The rules may be more relaxed and the rent higher but those areas which remain as allotments are still governed by the book of Rules & Regulations. The Village Green generates no income and its maintenance and upkeep depend on grants and fund-raising. Widely used for community events, it is an immense asset to the village.

The Green during the annual Scarecrow Weekenc: As the event has grown in popularity, it has raised more and more for village societies and for the upkeep of village amenities – such as The Green itself.

Time Off

Music on The Green in 2008.

Lubenham Playing Fields

After the Second World War it was decided to use some of the money raised from dances, whist drives and other fund-raising to provide a playing field and equipment for the children of the village. In 1949 £100 was paid for Tom Knight's Close, a half-acre field behind The Green and four Trustees (George Burditt, John Stubbs, David Fox and the Rev. Moffat Peake) became the joint tenants for 'the purpose of a recreation and pleasure ground for the Parish of Lubenham'. It was officially opened on Saturday 5 May 1951 by Major Guy Paget and since then subsequent trustees have raised money to maintain and upgrade the site and its equipment.

Public Houses

Lubenham used to have two public houses, *The Paget Arms* and *The Coach and Horses*.

Built in the 19th century when it was known as *The Red Cow*, *The Paget Arms* ceased trading in 1961. During World War II it was a popular venue for servicemen, especially the GIs, probably because it was a free house and had more choice of beers and spirits. Both pubs opened at 6.00pm and closed at 10.00pm with long queues forming before opening time.

Don Johnson recalls *'as a young boy I was not old enough to realise what was happening when the Americans exchanged white fivers for bottles of whisky. Black marketing was unknown to me!'*

A table top from *The Paget Arms*, carved mainly with the names of British and American servicemen, now hangs in *The Coach and Horses*. Known as *The White Swan* until the mid 19th century, *The Coach and Horses* dates from at least 1700 and was formerly a coaching inn. It is a popular meeting place for locals and holds regular quiz, darts and music nights.

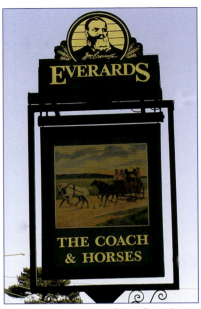

Sports clubs

As well as the many clubs and societies which meet regularly in the pub and Village Hall, there are sports clubs some of which date back several years.

Lubenham Cricket Club

Played on the field in front of the Old Hall, cricket was popular in the village before World War II with Lubenham winning the Fernie Monday Country Cup in 1936, 1937 and 1938, making it their own. After the War the club presented the cup to the Memorial Committee to be played for yearly by teams in the district, the funds raised going towards the upkeep of the War Memorial. Cricket was popular in the village during the 1950s and 60s, the team being dominated by such names as Ernie, George, Cecil and Albert Davis, Stan Johnson and Evan Neal, with George Burditt as president. The club disbanded in 1971 but was reformed in 1997–8 and now enjoys friendly matches with local teams. There are around 25 members who play their home games in the picturesque setting of Thorpe Lubenham Hall grounds.

Time Off

A Lubenham cricket team of the 1950s: Back row, left to right: Mr Martin, Stan Johnson, Charlie Chase, Albert Davis, Reg Perks, Ellis Howard, Ray Howard, Bill Howard (scorer); front row: Alan Howard, Charlie Pelos, George Davis, Len Weston, Ernie Davis.

A game in the field in front of Thorpe Lubenham Hall.

Football

Football has never taken hold in the village in the same way as cricket. There was a team in the late 1920s which reformed for a short time after World War II, playing on a field on Laughton Road, but it has since disbanded.

Lubenham Football Club 1920–21. Back row: F. Piper, G. Newman, J. Cockerill, J. Smith, —, W.R. Reynolds, J. Harris, W. Howard, E. Mutton.
Middle: O. Burditt, H. Patrick, G. May, C. Webb, E. Carter, N. Burditt.
Front: E. Neale, V. Sargeant, H. Newman, J. Carter, R. Ashton.

Lubenham Football Club early 1950s. Back row: Bill Faulkner, Tom Reynolds, Stan Johnson, Gerry Grant, Jack Moore, Reg Perks, – Monk, Monty Connell.
Front row: Jock Murray, – Monk, Charlie Harris, Arthur Rogers, Alan Howard, –.

Time Off

Lubenham Football Club 1961. Organised by Mr Coe of School Lane, the team only lasted a few seasons. Back row: – , Dennis Holton, Peter Robinson, Roy Hilyard, John Gilbert, Pat Cook. Front row: Len Tyler, John Harris, – , Ray Gerlach, Mick Hurley, Dave Burditt.

Cycling

In the 1990s, a group of villagers decided to take some regular exercise by cycling around the local area. Their friendly get-togethers developed into the Lubenham Raiders Cycling Club with around 50 participants meeting regularly in the summer for organised rides of 10 to 20 miles, ending their journey at *The Coach and Horses* for a well earned drink and refreshments! Some of the hardier members even arrange week-long trips in other parts of the country and abroad.

International cyclo-cross and mountain bike champion Vic Barnett of Lubenham

Vic began riding in local cyclo-cross events in 1959. In 1972 he was selected to represent Great Britain at the World Championships in Prague. This was the start of his international career in which he represented Britain on numerous occasions, including five years as a professional.

Later he turned his attention to mountain biking and won the World Masters Championship in Montreal in 2000 and 2001. He became British Masters Cyclo-cross Champion in 2000 and the World Masters Champion in 2005 when he took the title in a sprint finish. In 2011 he was undefeated British Masters champion in both cyclo-cross and mountain biking and in 2012 won the World Masters Cyclo-Cross Championship held in Louisville, Kentucky.

Cycling has taken him all over the world from Belgium to Brazil, Australia to America. He has won numerous Sports Personality of the Year awards from the *Leicester Mercury* and *Harborough Mail*.

Rifle club

In 1930 Col. Wernher applied to convert the former pickle factory in Rushes Lane into a rifle range and a Miniature Rifle Club was formed. It closed a few years later.

Time Off

The Scarecrows

In 2001 two friends, Clare Johnson and Mary Gilkes, decided to raise funds for All Saints Church by organising a Weekend of Straw. From these relatively low-key beginnings, Lubenham's Scarecrow Festival has developed into an event attracting thousands of visitors each year and raising money for local charities and organisations. As well as around 100 original and often highly amusing scarecrows, there are traditional stalls, games and fairground rides on the Village Green, vintage vehicle displays, tractor and trailer rides and many other attractions.

Special Commemorations

The Scarecrow Festival epitomises the strong sense of community in Lubenham. People work together, form committees, help on the day and make scarecrows. The same is true when commemorating events of national importance, including royal occasions such as a coronation, wedding or jubilee.

The Lubenham Victory Day celebration was held on 8 June 1946. The day started at 10.00am with a Thanksgiving Service in the parish church conducted by the Assistant Bishop of Leicester who later judged the Best Decorated House Competition. After lunch a children's Fancy Dress Parade was held in the park at Thorpe Lubenham followed by sports for children and adults, with accompanying side shows and competitions. Children's teas were served in the school at 4.30pm – 'children must bring their own cups'! A social evening for adults, with games, competitions and dancing, was held in the Unionist Hall.

In June 1946 a committee was established to raise money to move the War Memorial from Main Street opposite Westgate Lane to its present site and create a memorial garden. The names of those killed during the Second World War were also added. Committee minutes reveal the huge amount of work undertaken to raise funds by organising many dances, raffles,

Above: Village celebrations for the coronation of George VI and Queen Elizabeth in 1937 included a fancy dress competition, won by Bernard Patrick and his sister Audrey. **Below:** Lubenham celebrates victory in World War Two in true British style – a social evening at the Unionist Hall (now the Village Hall).

LUBENHAM

CORONATION
FESTIVITIES

PROGRAMME:

10 a.m. **Service** (Open Air if fine).

1 p.m. **Luncheon,** in Covered Court at Thorpe Lubenham Hall,
by kind permission of Sir Harold and Lady Zia Wernher.

2.30 p.m. **Fancy Dress Parade** (Children) no Dress to cost more than 2/6
Decorated Bicycles (Prizes given).

3 p.m. **Sports for all in the Park.**

4.30 p.m. **Children's Tea** (and Presentation of Souvenir Mugs).

5 p.m. **Sports continued.**

9 p.m. **Dance in Unionist Hall, SAVANA BAND.**

Prizes for Best Decorated **DWELLING-HOUSE,**
First Prize 10/-; Second 7/6; Third 5/-.

NOTICE.

There may be a few residents who have not yet subscribed, but are desirous of doing so. Will any such persons please hand their donations as soon as possible to any of the following: Nurse Hunt, Mr. G. Ashby, Mr. J. Carter, Mr. F. Burnham, Mr. G. Burditt or Mr. Piper.

Persons who have not subscribed may not be invited to the Lunch.

Tickets will be issued to all Adults (14 years and over), on application to Mrs. E. PAYNE.

Tickets for Children's Tea will be issued by Miss BATTY.

There will be a Buffet for Adults requiring Tea in the afternoon on payment.

Admission to Dance, Free, also Refreshments, by Ticket from Mrs. BURNHAM.

Old Age Pensioners will have a gift of Tea or Tobacco on handing in their names to NURSE HUNT, not later than APRIL 18th.

Green & Co., Printers, Market Harborough.

Lubenham celebrates the Coronation: wet weather in 1953 marked the big day, just as it did 60 years later when the village celebrated the Diamond Jubilee. However, on both days people made the best of it – although in 2012 there was no gift of tobacco offered to pensioners!

Sixty years on, the Village Hall was again at the centre of five days of celebrations, with a photographic display marking the Diamond Jubilee. An official portrait of Queen Elizabeth and Prince Philip was unveiled by Lady Caroline MacPhail. She is pictured with (from left) Len Bale, the chairman of the Village Hall Committee; William Noble (9) of All Saints Primary School, who designed the cover of the jubilee programme; and Terry Cain, chairman of Lubenham Diamond Jubilee Committee.

sales and whist drives. The War Memorial was officially unveiled on the new site on 23 April 1950 by Major Guy Paget.

Celebrations for the Coronation of Queen Elizabeth II on 2 June 1953 followed a remarkably similar pattern to those of Victory Day eight years earlier. The official poster outlines the programme (see opposite). However, one resident recalls that the day was so wet many people stayed in the Village Hall, squinting at a hastily erected and minute television set!

Queen Elizabeth's Silver, Golden and Diamond Jubilees were each commemorated by a weekend of activity carefully planned so that everyone, whatever their age or interests, could take part. Events such as exhibitions, treasure hunts, cricket matches, fun races, disco or barn dances and picnics on The Green were well supported with villagers taking part with enthusiasm.

A similar event was organised to honour the Queen's Diamond Jubilee in June 2012. As with the Coronation Day the wet weather did not spoil proceedings.

Lubenham Village History

Above: A beacon was lit on Mill Hill, one of a planned chain of more than 2012 beacons across the UK, Channel Islands, Isle of Man, the Commonwealth and UK Overseas Territories to celebrate the Diamond Jubilee on Monday 4th June.
Below: The programme for the jubilee celebrations.

Lubenham Diamond Jubilee
Five Days of Celebrations

Friday 1st June in the Village Hall

- 6.30pm — **Photograph Display**
  Children's Portraits
  Refreshments
  Unveiling of the portrait of HM the Queen.
  (Free Admission)

- 7.30 – 10pm — **Film Show**
  by Harborough Movie Makers
  (Free Admission)

Saturday 2nd June at the Coach and Horses

- 8.30 – 10.30am **Diamond Jubilee Breakfast**

Saturday 2nd June in the Village Hall

- 10am – 4pm — **Photograph Display**
  Children's Portraits
  (Free Admission)

- 7.30pm — **Barn Dance**
  Admission by ticket only
  (£10 per head to include Fish and Chip Supper, Bar)

Sunday 3rd June at the Church

- 10am — **Special Jubilee Service**

Sunday 3rd June in the Village Hall

- 12noon – 5pm — **Photograph Display**
  Children's Portraits
  (Free Admission)

Sunday 3rd June on the Village Green

- 12.30 – 5pm — **The Big Jubilee Lunch**
  Bring your own picnic (food and bar also available) and listen to music by Harborough Band and Songbirds Ladies Choir. The Songbirds will be singing from 2.00pm till 2.45pm
  Harborough Band will be playing two sessions between 3.00pm and 5.00pm.
  Incidental music Mr Stephen Hancock.
  (Free Admission) All times are approximate

Monday 4th June

- 10.00am — **Church Bells ringing**

Monday 4th June on the Village Green

- 2-5pm — **Family Fun Day**
  Activities Sideshows and Demonstrations throughout the afternoon. Tug of War and Bar.
  Main display area times.
  2pm The Harborough Gymnasts
  2.30pm The Bakanalia Border Morris Side
  2.30pm The Tug of War commences
  3.00pm The Army Cadets Display
  (Free Admission) All times are approximate

Monday 4th June in the Village Hall 2-5 Photos & Refreshments

- 10.15pm — **Lighting the Beacon on Mill Hill**
  Viewing from the Village Green

Tuesday 5th June on the Village Green

- 11am – 5.00pm — **Old Style Village Fayre**
  Demonstrations of Rural Crafts.
  Food, Bar and Craft Stalls
  (Free Admission)

For a place to sit down, head for the Village Hall where tea, coffee and biscuits will be served on Saturday, Sunday and Monday during the photograph display and children's portraits exhibition.

Rosemary Slough

10. Horses and hunting

What do the National Hunt Chase, a 19th century Grand National winner, one of the most famous racehorses of the 20th century and International Events riders have in common? The answer is Lubenham. The surrounding area has long been associated with horses and hunting, which have influenced the history, architecture, employment and social life of the village.

In the 19th century especially, the wealthy and influential were attracted to the district during the hunting season when they rode with the Fernie, Pytchley and other nearby hunts. Jack 'Cherry' Angell[1] not only spent much time here but employed nationally known architects to convert two former Georgian farm houses into hunting boxes where he could entertain his many guests.[2] Lord Hopetoun, whose grand ancestral home and 6,500 acre estate is situated near Edinburgh, purchased Papillon Hall in 1866 but died of typhoid aged 42 after what has been described as a brief life devoted to Paris and the Pytchley Hunt! Sir Harold and Lady Zia Wernher had a string of polo ponies, race horses and hunters at Thorpe Lubenham Hall during the 1920s and 1930s. The Paget family, who owned Lubenham Lodge, were well known on the hunting field, with Guy being Master of the Pytchley for many years and his son, Reginald, following in his footsteps. In addition, many local farmers and gentry owned horses on which they rode to hounds or took part in point-to-points.

Horse power for transport and farming was essential in a rural area until the expansion of mechanisation during World War II. As a result, many in the village were employed working with horses as farm labourers, coachmen, wagoners and

Above: A painting of Jack 'Cherry' Angel (in red jacket) and John Gore.
Below: Aerial view of Gore Lodge and stableyard in the 1950s.

Horses & Hunting

grooms. According to the 1891 Census, Gore Lodge alone employed five grooms. A groom would not only look after the horses, often living in accommodation above the stables, but would ride a hack to the meet leading the hunters for owners who followed in carriages. Later, horses and grooms would be transported by train in specially adapted carriages. The rail network meant that horses, riders and hunt followers could be conveyed further distances in a shorter time. There is a story from 1930s about the Reverend Graham Dilley, known locally as 'The Hunting Parson', who after returning home by train with his horses created a hue and cry that his car had been stolen, until he was reminded that his horses had indeed travelled by train but that he himself had driven to the meet in his car which was still in Melton Mowbray!

Blacksmiths were a vital part of the local economy, not only shoeing the many horses but repairing and making tackle, tools and farm implements. At various times there were forges at *The Coach and Horses*, on Main Street opposite Westgate Lane, Rose Cottage and in Rushes Lane. The 1891 Census lists five people in Lubenham employed as blacksmiths. Monty Connell, who died in 1987, was the last farrier in the village, working in Rushes Lane.

The importance of horses is shown by the number of stables in the 19th century. Gore Lodge and The Cottage (later the Tower House) were hunting boxes owned by Jack Angell and each had a coach house and stabling for 12 horses. Thorpe Lubenham Hall was even larger, with 18 stables, five double coach houses, wash box, harness and feed rooms and groom's accommodation. Other substantial stable blocks

> A legend persists that *Alcibiade* is buried in the garden of the Tower House next to the Church wall. Unfortunately, no remains have ever been found to substantiate the story.

were found at The Laurels and Manor Farm and *The Coach and Horses*, a former coaching inn, had three stalls, a loose box, carriage house and blacksmith's workshop. In addition, every farm would have had stables or barns for its working horses, together with feed stores and wagon hovels. Development continued into the 20th century. The Mill House was used as a livery yard from 1972 to 1998, principally to keep hunters for their owners and produce young horses for showing and eventing. Twenty-four stables and a cross-country course were built at Lubenham Lodge and by the early 2000s the Lodge was at times the base for International Events riders such as Oliver Townend and Georgina 'Piggy' French. Holmes Farm has around 20 stables, an indoor school and horse walker, mainly for private 'do-it-yourself' owners. Lubenham's long association with horses and riding still continues.

Now displayed in Harborough Museum, the stable door contains horseshoes from famous horses associated with Lubenham, including *Bridegroom*, *Alcibiade* and *Queensferry*.

Head groom Dalton Wetherill holding *Brown Jack* (on the right) and stable companion *Mail Fist*. Also pictured is groom Bill Wilford.

Famous horses associated with Lubenham

In 1865 five-year-old *Alcibiade*, owned by Jack Angell, won the Grand National at odds of 100–7. Ridden by Capt. Henry Coventry and trained by a Mr Cornell this French-bred horse remains one of the youngest-ever winners of the race.

Bridegroom and *Queensferry*, both owned by Jack Angell, were the first two winners of the Grand National Hunt Steeple Chase. Originally intended by his previous owner to be a Grand National contender, *Bridegroom*, ridden by Edmund Charles (Doughey) Burton of Daventry, won the inaugural race in 1860 by 20 lengths for the substantial prize of £500. *Bridegroom* went on to win several other prestigious races and was fourth and second respectively in the 1861 and 1862 Liverpool Grand Nationals. *Queensferry*, also racing in Angell's distinctive colours of cherry with yellow spots, won the 1861 race by 30 lengths but failed in other races that year.

Brown Jack was bought by Sir Harold and Lady Zia Wernher as a three-year-old in 1927 for 750 guineas. He spent his first season racing over hurdles, winning seven out of ten starts including the Ascot Stakes and Champion Hurdles. However, the following year his trainer, Aubrey Hastings, switched to racing on the flat and with his regular jockey, Steve Donoghue, *Brown Jack* captured the public imagination by winning the three-mile Queen Alexandra Stakes for six consecutive years. In 1930 he also won the prestigious Goodwood and Doncaster Cups. The website horseracing.co.uk names him amongst the top ten race horses of all time, a list which includes such legends as *Arkle*, *Nijinsky*, *Seabiscuit*, *Red Rum* and *Best Mate*.

> *Brown Jack* had a number of idiosyncrasies, one of which was to sit on his manger to have his hooves shod! After retirement he spent the rest of his life in stable 13 at Thorpe Lubenham Hall. He died the night before he was to be moved to Luton Hoo.

The National Hunt Chase

This acclaimed horse race held every year at the celebrated Cheltenham Festival actually started life as the Grand National Hunt Steeple Chase in fields at the bottom of Rushes Lane in Lubenham. Prominent trainer Dr Fothergill Rowlands suggested setting up a new four-mile steeple chase in response to the precarious state of jump racing at the time. The racecourse was required to simulate true hunting conditions, with natural fences and sections of plough and ridge and furrow. The inaugural race, with a field of 31 horses, was held on Wednesday 18 April 1860 as part of the Market Harborough meeting and the panel of stewards read like a *Who's Who*: The

---

LAWRENCE'S CORRECT LIST.

(PUBLISHED BY AUTHORITY.)

THE

GRAND NATIONAL HUNT

AND

MARKET HARBOROUGH

STEEPLE CHASES,

ON WEDNESDAY, THE 18th OF APRIL, 1860.

STEWARDS OF THE NATIONAL HUNT STEEPLE CHASE.

HIS GRACE THE DUKE OF BEAUFORT.	SIR WATKIN W. WYNN, BART.
HIS GRACE THE DUKE OF MANCHESTER.	THE HON. GEORGE LANE FOX.
RIGHT HON. THE EARL OF STAMFORD AND WARRINGTON.	T. T. DRAKE, ESQ.
	W. R. STRETTON, ESQ.
RIGHT HON. THE EARL OF SCARBORO'.	W. W. TAILBY, ESQ.
RIGHT HON. LORD DACRE.	W. H. POWELL, ESQ.
RIGHT HON. LORD TREDEGAR.	

STEWARDS OF THE MARKET HARBOROUGH STEEPLE CHASES.

LORD BATEMAN.	HON. F. W. C. VILLIERS.
LORD CURZON.	W. S. CRAWFURD, ESQ.
THE HON. C. CUST.	W. W. TALBY, ESQ.

JUDGE.
MR. CLARK, Newmarket.

CLERK OF THE COURSE,	HONORARY SECRETARY,
MR. T. MARSHALL, Northampton.	MR. J. FLINT, Market Harborough.

CONDITIONS.

The decision of the Stewards to be final on all matters connected with the Steeple Chases, and not subject to any appeal to a Court of Law.

Five horses to start for each Race, or the money added will not be given.

The usual conditions of Steeple Chasing will be strictly observed.

Any objection to be made in writing before starting, or the same will not be entertained.

Admission to the Ground—Saddle Horse, 1/; Carriage with one Horse, 2/; Carriage with pair of Horses, 3/; Carriage with four Horses, 5/.—No one will be allowed on the Ground or in the Fields adjoining to sell refreshments without tickets of admission.

2.0—The Grand National Hunt Steeple Chase,

A Sweepstakes of 10 sovs. each, 5 sovs. forfeit, which must be sent with the nomination, with a sum not exceeding £500 added; to be collected from the different Hunts in the Country; the second horse to receive £50 out of the stakes; for horses that have never won before the day of starting, 12st. each. Four miles over a fair hunting country. To be ridden by Gentlemen, Members of any established Hunt,—by Members of any Club elected by ballot, by Officers in the Army, Navy, Militia, or Volunteers,—or by Farmers occupying at least 100 acres of land, and who have never ridden for hire. The Winner to pay 20 sovs. towards the expenses.

1	Mr. Adam's Woodman ..	
2	Mr. F. Allen's Kaffir ..	*green, white cap*
3	Mr. B. F. Angell's b h Borderer, aged	*cherry, yellow spots*
4	———— b h Bridegroom, aged	*cherry, yellow spots*
5	Major Baker's b h Golden Branch, by Weatherbit, out of Moose Deer, a,	*blue & white stripes*
6	Lord Bateman's br h Marshal Saxe, aged	*black and rose, rose sleeves*
7	———— br h Kilkenny, aged ..	*black and rose, rose sleeves*
8	Mr. Barber's Miss Harkaway ..	*brown, white cap*
9	Mr. J. Bennett's b g Ringleader	*crimson, black belt and cap*
10	Mr. H. Blundell's Dutch Drops	*purple*

Duke of Beaufort, the Duke of Manchester, the Earl of Stamford and Warrington, the Earl of Scarborough, Lord Dacre and Lord Tredegar amongst others. Every hunt in the country was expected to contribute £10 to the race. The race card clearly defined who could ride: gentlemen, members of any established Hunt, members of any Club elected by ballot, Officers in the Army, Navy, Militia or Volunteers or farmers occupying at least 100 acres of land.

18 April was a clear day with a cold north-easterly wind. Market Harborough was brimming with people, many buildings were decorated and the town was filled with itinerant travellers selling their wares. The crowd was estimated at 40,000, many of whom crowded on the vantage point of Farndon Hill. The race itself took place on land belonging to Mr Stratford of Lubenham on an area lying parallel to the Rugby to Stamford railway line consisting of pasture and ridge and furrow with hedges, ditches and man-made sheep hurdles and fences. One significant feature was the brook, about half a mile from home, which was said to be about 15 feet wide with a row of thorns three feet high on the take-off side. The winner was *Bridegroom* owned by Jack 'Cherry' Angell.

The Grand National Hunt Steeple Chase was held in Lubenham the following year and again in 1863 on a slightly different course. The race subsequently moved to other venues before finally settling at the Cheltenham Festival in 1911.

References

[1] See Chapter 7, *Village characters*.
[2] See Chapter 6, *Mansions and cottages*.

The famous Victorian courtesan Catherine 'Skittles' Walters, whose many suitors included the then Prince of Wales and Lord Hartington, heir to the Duke of Devonshire, was a daring horsewoman who reportedly easily cleared the difficult 15 feet water jump for £100 bet after all other riders had failed.

11. Tales of Papillon Hall

The site of Papillon Hall stands on a spur of land above the River Welland about one mile west of Lubenham. The Hall itself was demolished in the early 1950s but remains a place of mystery.[1]

Tales of ghosts, apparitions and strange noises in the night centre on David Papillon (1691–1762), known as Old Pamp, the great grandson of the Hall's founder. It appears that David was universally hated and feared in the area. Accounts abound of how he would hypnotise people, such as the occasion when men working in a field so angered him that he 'fixed' them, so they were unable to move until he released them later that day.

The most famous story is that of the Spanish mistress and her cursed slippers. David Papillon was reported to have a mistress who he kept locked in the east attic, a room which could only be entered by crawling on hands and knees. She could be seen walking regularly on the flat roof between the gables but mysteriously disappeared just before Old Pamp was due to marry. Legend has it that he poisoned her but that before she died, she cursed her fine green slippers. Evil would befall if the slippers in which she wanted to walk ever left the House. A skeleton of a woman, reportedly found during alterations to the east attic in 1903, added to the mystery. The story gained so much credence over the years that the slippers, when found walled up in the building, were handed to each new owner with the deeds.

Tales of the cursed slippers proliferated in the 19th century. Were they true or was it the Victorian love of ghost and horror stories that caused this sudden interest? In one incident, when Lord Hopetoun owned the Hall, the whole household was woken by a resounding noise of furniture being thrown and shutters banging. When the door to the drawing room was opened the noise ceased and the room remained undisturbed. Lord Hopetoun immediately retrieved the slippers from the daughter of a previous owner and the incidents temporarily ceased. The next householder, Thomas Halford, sent the shoes to the Paris Exhibition for a whole year but life was purportedly so intolerable that the Halford family left the house. Aware of the rumours, his successor Mr Walker, installed a small fireproof safe with iron grid and padlock in which the slippers were secured.

The locked grille installed to house the 'cursed' slippers.

Captain Frank Bellville despatched the shoes to his solicitor for safekeeping when alterations to the Hall were carried out in 1903/04. Several incidents occurred whilst they were away, including a builder killed by a falling brick, Bellville sustaining a broken skull when his pony and trap bolted and lightening setting fire to a stable block, killing three ponies. Were these episodes mere coincidence or the result of the curse? More recently, the owners of the farm on the site have also experienced noise of furniture being thrown around in the night only to find everything normal and in place in the morning.

What is the reality behind these tales? There is no factual evidence that David Papillon had a mistress, Spanish or otherwise. He married Mary Keyser, the daughter of a wealthy merchant, and moved to Acrise in Kent where they appear to have had a long and happy life together. He was the Member of Parliament for Dover for many years.

The slippers and one patten (protective overshoe) still exist and are stored by the Leicestershire Museums Services. Although faded with age, they are exquisite; made of green silk brocade glued over white leather with heels of red leather. They were described as Spanish in origin by the British Museum in 1952 but this identification is in doubt. It is now known that trade routes with China were better established than previously thought and that silk was more common. These shoes could be Spanish, Italian, French or indeed English.

The Papillon slippers dating from the early 18th century. Also shown is one patten or overshoe.

The fact that they were found walled up has always given credence to 'the curse of the slippers' story. However, there are many superstitions associated with shoes, including that they were signs of good luck, and research has shown that it was

108

common practice to hide them in this way with footwear having been found in buildings of all types, ages and in various parts of the world.[2] The expensive Papillon slippers are unusual in that they were in a good condition and not worn or broken as is normally the case.

Another mysterious tale of Papillon Hall is centred on the picture of David, Old Pamp, which is said to hypnotise the viewer, come out of the frame and haunt the place where it is hanging. It is a portrait of David Papillon aged 24, painted by an unidentified artist in 1715. Its current whereabouts are unknown. Even though the Papillon family had sold the house 76 years previously the picture remained at the Hall until 1840 when the then owner Mr Marriott begged Thomas Papillon to take it away. Marriott claimed his servants were too frightened to stay as Old Pamp came out of the frame and haunted the house. At some point the Papillon family moved from Kent to Crowhurst Place in East Sussex and by the turn of the 20th century Crowhurst was rented to a Col. Tufnell and his family. The Tufnells knew nothing of the stories emanating from Papillon Hall but letters, now in Leicestershire Records Office, from Mrs Bertha Tufnell reveal the extent of fear surrounding the portrait in the drawing room. She said she could not pass the picture without being compelled to stare at it for a long time and that others had the same experience. Old Pamp reportedly came out of his frame and at one point followed her sister-in-law who claimed she could 'feel his cold hands around her neck trying to throttle her'. For whatever reason, the influence of the portrait or mounting hysteria, Mrs Tufnell wrote to Pelham Papillon, begging him to remove the painting. Mr Pettitt, an employee at Crowhurst, made a strong wooden case in which to transport the picture but by coincidence, the night before it was to be moved, Pettitt drowned in the well.

David Papillon (1691–1762) aged 24, known as 'Old Pamp'.
He was said to come out of his frame and haunt the house.

Today, many people still believe the legends surrounding Papillon Hall. Others are more sceptical, but either way, they are fascinating tales and a part of the tradition and heritage of Lubenham.

References
[1] See Chapter 6, *Mansions and cottages*.
[2] Swann, June. *Shoes concealed in buildings*. Costume, no. 30, 1996.

Appendix: Lubenham in the early 1900s

John Carter (1898 – 1991) lived in Lubenham all his life and researched and recorded the history of the village for over 70 years. The following extracts from his writings have been reproduced by kind permission of his sons, John and David.

NB: [ ] indicate editor's notes.

MANY CHANGES have taken place in the village during the present [20th] century. Quite a number of old cottages have been demolished and many more have been built, and anyone who left the village before the First World War coming back would hardly recognise it.

First of all, the Parish of Lubenham extended from Plowman's Nursery [near the present day roundabout on Lubenham Hill] to Scoborough crossing on the Theddingworth Road, and in my early boyhood days about 1904 there wasn't a single house between Lubenham village and Plowman's house and nursery at the Coventry road corner. Welland Park didn't exist, it was just open fields, and in Lubenham, coming along the main road from Harboro', there was a thatched cottage on the left-hand side next to the Hollies, called Beehive Cottage. This was demolished in 1965 to give more space to Sunny Court, which incidentally, was a stable with stabling for 15/20 horses before its conversion to living accommodation after the Second World War. Just ahead on the right was the blacksmith's forge, owned by Mr Alf Newman. This was a butcher's shop in the 19th Century owned by Mr J. Ellson who gave to a section of the villagers the piece of ground in the corner of his paddock on which the Independent Chapel was built in 1838.

We then come to the village pond which was walled in with an entrance and exit opening either side, so that the cattle being driven to Harborough market from the villages could walk in and drink. There was a pump at the front of the pond with a stone trough so that dogs could quench their thirst.

Next to the pond and standing back from the road were two thatched cottages [demolished in the 1930s] that looked a picture with the background of the trees. Over the road, next to the shop, was a bake house, a long thatched house with a holly hedge in front of it. This was demolished about the same period and the present houses built by Sir Harold Wernher for his workmen. In those days the villagers would take their joint of meat and Yorkshire pudding to the bake house on Sundays mornings to be baked and around 1pm there would be an exodus from the pubs to the bake house to collect them. The aroma was as good as a feast and the charge for this service was 1d.

I should have mentioned that before we got to the bake house we passed the *Coach and Horses Inn*. This shows a date of 1700 but this was probably the date it was 'modernised' as a beam over a doorway inside shows a date of 1670.

Now we come to *The Paget Arms*, no longer an inn, but in the old days was known as *The Red Cow*. This became the property of the Paget family in the middle of the 19th century when they acquired quite a large slice of the village. It was getting rather dilapidated, so was modernised and renamed *The Paget Arms*. It was a free house.

Cross the Rushes Lane junction and come to a row of dwellings known as The Barracks with a shop that in those days was a butcher's shop. Next a short brick wall, then a row of six brick and slated cottages [now a block of flats] and then a paddock that went with Western Villa, a residence that stood on the corner of Westgate Lane [demolished c.1970].

On the opposite side of the main road was the turn to Laughton and Foxton. These were gated roads, three gates on the Laughton road and four to Foxton, no houses at all. The first gate to Laughton was almost a monopoly of the Westgate Lane kids on Tuesdays. Quite a few farmers from Laughton and Mowsley used to go to the Harboro' market in their pony-traps, and threw pennies when the children opened the gate for them, and in the afternoon on their return, if they had done good business in the market and were a bit tipsy, it might be a shilling or even half a crown. That was a lot of money in those days. Foxton wasn't so profitable as they used the other road more than ours.

Let us continue our journey along the main road past Westgate Lane and we come to a cottage on our left. This used to be two tenements, one as a small shop for knick-knacks and sweets for children. I remember buying a Jew's harp for a penny but never mastered the art of playing it properly. On the opposite side of the road were open fields until after the Second World War.

Proceeding along the road we come to a culvert and bridge over a streamlet that joins the river Welland near the Washpit. That bridge was known as Peter-stone Bridge, as near it one could find the star stones. These stones are fossilized stems of crinoids or sea-lilies and are over 150 million years old. The Washpit was in a small field nearby and my father used to wash several thousand sheep every year. Sheep washing took place in early May, just before shearing, and to raise the water level, planks were dropped into slots at the sides of the dam. A wooden 'tub' structure was fixed to cross beams in which my father stood and, as the sheep were thrown into the pit and ducked with a special pole, my father would grab them one at a time and hold them under the spout of water, turning them over and over.

Next we come to the railway bridge and the station on the right. This was the L&NW railway line to Rugby.

We must now re-trace our steps and turn left to go round The Green. Not much has changed here until we get to the entrance to Mill Hill where a new house was built around 1930 by Mr A. Marvell. Next to number 47 The Green two small cottages stood back from the road [demolished 1920s] and opposite them was a pump. Next to them was another thatched block of three tenements built 1668 [demolished 1972]. Lower down there were three small cottages dated W.G.1833 [now partially demolished]. Then comes the Vicarage, believed to be the remains of an old fortified manor. Just ahead and facing us is the present Manor House built in mid 18th Century [?] by John Wright. To the left is Underhill Road. This was the route taken by the farm wagons to take corn up to the mill for grinding as Mill Hill was too steep. We turn right and on our left is a thatched house, probably early 18th century, a farmhouse originally and later the bake house was built onto it. The thatch was removed and the whole block slated for safety when the bake house was added. Next comes Rose Cottage, already mentioned. This blacksmith's shop was a hive of industry and it was a thrill for we lads to watch the proceedings and see the sparks fly as the red hot bar was hammered into shape, and the clouds of pungent smoke billowing out as the horseshoe was placed on the hoof.

Now we cross the main road and go down School Lane. On the right is 'The House that Jack Built' and on the left The White House. This was a dairy farm occupied by Mr W.H. Vendy. I remember a mud-walled shed with a thatched roof stood in the paddock about halfway along the lane, the walls were a foot or more thick, so the farmstead must have been very old. I am inclined to think it may have been the old *Three Crowns Inn*, mentioned in the Constable's records dated 1746.

Further down the lane on the left was the Perkins' factory, where black plush was made for hats and later they made embroidery for railway carriage upholstery. Next to the factory was a row of small cottages for some of the work people. Next to them was the factory yard with the boiler house and two gasometers where the Perkins' made their own gas and supplied their houses in the village. Adjoining the yard was an area of gardens for tenants of the cottages, then a paddock that was referred to as the Crowfield. In this paddock were several tall elm trees. Every year these trees were crowded with rooks nests and after nesting was over, they used to shoot the crows and sell them at 6d for four, and crow pie was on many a table during this period.

On the opposite side of the road was a thatched cottage, a double gate leading to the stable yard of the Tower House and a carpenter's shop [demolished 1938]. Next to that was a thatched cottage [demolished 1920s]. A little further along we come to the school on the left with its playground walled all round and the school house attached. On the opposite side of the road was the garden to the block called Bird's Corner opposite Old Hall Lane. The first small dwelling was a thatched and timbered cottage with lath and daub in-filling, butting onto a brick house on a stone base [demolished 1972].

Round the corner in Church Walk on the right hand side of the lane is the timbered house of cruck construction with thatched roof, an addition to the original building is dated 1731. Opposite stand a pair of dwellings occupied by Mr George Burditt and a member of the Sprigg family. At the top of the lane near the church is a small thatched cottage and opposite a brick and slated building dated 1737 used as a vicarage in the early 20th century when the Rev A.R. Miles and Rev C.C. Allen were rectors.

Going through the churchyard we come to Rushes Lane and on our right is the Tower House. Further along on the left, just beyond Adam's Farm, stood a row of small thatched and ivy-covered cottages [demolished 1956].

Further along and on the same side was the Ketchup factory where the Perkins family used to make sauces. On the opposite side of the road is the smithy, always busy with the numerous hunters stabled in the village as well as the farm horse, also agricultural implements that required repair and maintenance.

To complete our tour of the village we get onto the main road and go on our left until we come to Westgate Lane on the left. On the corner stands Western Villa, already mentioned, the outbuildings of which abut the lane. Then there is a row of cottages of late 18th or early 19th century construction with a passage to the backs and gardens, and next to that several old cottages, one or two with thatched roofs. On the opposite side of the road is a block of three small dwellings and a row going off at a tangent known as Workhouse Cottages and down at the corner a block of two small cottages at the entrance to Brooksbank Lane [Washpit Lane].

On the corner was the pump to supply drinking water for the cottages at the lower end of Westgate Lane. The lane leading onto Rushes Lane and the Church was called Buswell's Lane and had fir trees on either side.

That ends our tour of the village in the first decade of the 20th Century.

Lubenham village history

List of illustrations

(listed by page number)

Reproduced by kind permission of the following:

Leicestershire County Council: *(bottom)* 29, *(top & middle)* 42, 43, *(bottom)* 44, 75, 107, 108, 109

LCC Harborough Museum: *(top)* 44, *(bottom)* 79, *(top)* 80

Market Harborough Historical Society: *(bottom)* 30

Records Office for Leicester, Leicestershire & Rutland: 105, 106

Leicester Mercury: *(bottom)* 67

Andrew Carpenter: 99, 100

David Carter: 13, *(top)* 16, 27, 37, 38, 39, 40, 45, *(top)* 67, *(top)* 46, *(top)* 47, *(middle)* 48, *(middle)* 50, 54, *(top)* 55, *(top)* 57, 60, *(bottom)* 61, *(top)* 63, *(top & middle)* 64, *(top)* 67, *(top)* 68, 69, *(top)* 73, *(top)* 74, 77, *(bottom)* 80, *(top)* 81, *(top)* 91, 92, 95, 96, 104, 110, 111, *back cover*

Jonathan Clark: 8, *(bottom)* 14, *(top)*17, 18, *(bottom)* 49, 52, *(top)* 51, *(middle)* 53, *(bottom)* 63, *(bottom)* 68, *(middle)* 81, *(bottom)* 85, *(bottom)* 86, 87, 88, *(top)* 89, *(bottom)* 93, *front cover*

Lubenham Heritage Group: *(top)* 14, 15, *(bottom)* 17, *(top)* 19, 20, 26, *(top)* 29, *(top)* 30, 31, 32, 34, *(bottom)* 35, *(bottom)* 42, *(bottom)* 47, *(top & bottom)* 48, *(top)* 49, *(middle)* 50, *(top)* 51, *(top & bottom)* 53, *(bottom)* 55, *(top & middle)* 86, *(bottom)* 89, *(top)* 90, 103

Vic Barnett: 94

Jim Burbidge: *(bottom)* 57, *(top)* 61, 62, *(bottom)* 81

David Burditt: *(bottom)* 50, 65, *(top)* 93

John and Pat Dyke: 23, 24, 76

Geoff Ellis: 32, *(bottom)* 46, *(bottom)* 51, *(middle)* 55, *(top)* 79

David Hannibal: 102

Andrew Moore: *(bottom)* 74

June Moore: 28

Elizabeth Page: *(bottom)* 91

Bernard Patrick: 21, 84, 97

Michael Salter: *(bottom)* 16

Peter Shelton: ii, *(bottom)* 73

Rosemary Slough: *(bottom)* 90, 101

Elizabeth Wells: 1, 41

Eileen Wild: (top & mid) 35

Roger Wild: *(bottom)* 19

Don Wing: *(bottom)* 97, 98

Patricia Woods: 25, *(bottom)* 30, 85, 95, 96

Index

A

Adam's Farm 50, 60
Agriculture 57–62
  – Open-field system 57–58
  – Enclosures 59, 60
Airfield 23, 79–80
Airfield Farm Development 3, 4,
  13, 56
Alcibiade 74, 103–4
American Service Personnel 80–81, 90
Angell, Jack 'Cherry' 51, 52, 74, 101,
  102, 104
Anglo-Saxons 4, 13

B

Barnett, Vic 94
Baud family 6, 7
Baud's Manor (see also Old Hall) 6, 7,
  41, 47
Bellville, Frank 45, 75, 108
Bermingham, Isaac 59
Black Death 7
Blacksmiths 67, 103
Brooke, Sir Basil 8, 59–60
Brown Jack 46, 77, 104
Bullivant, Rev. H.E. 20, 30, 74–75

C

Carter, John 111–113
Chapel, The Independent &
  Congregational 32
Church, All Saints 20, 25–32
  – bells 31
  – churchyard 31
  – Mediaeval wall paintings 26–27
  – stained glass windows 30, 31, 79
  – Vestry meetings 9, 10, 12, 34
  – wall hanging 31
Coach & Horses 11, 15, 67, 68,
  90, 103
Cottage Estate v, 49, 52, 74
Council housing 55

C (cont.)

Cricket Club 90
Cycling 93
Cubitt, Messrs 51, 52
Cunard, Gordon 46, 76

D

Danelaw 4
Domesday survey 5
Dower House 48–49
Draper's House 50, 64

E

Eden House 47–48, 65
Edis, Robert William 52
Education (See also School)
  – history of 33, 36, 39–40
  – in Lubenham 33–40
Eldridge, Thomas 11, 34
Enclosure Act 9, 47, 59–60, 87

F

Factories
  – Britannia Mills, Coventry 71
  – Lingerie 52, 68,
  – Perkins (Victoria Mills) 12, 17,
  54, 69–71
Football Club 92–93
Foxton Locks 19
Freeholders 6, 8, 41, 47, 59

G

Garages 16–17, 66
Gore Lodge 52–53, 102–103
Grand National Hunt Steeple Chase
  105–106
Grand Union Canal 18–19
Green, no 49 53
Green Gardens 62, 74, 87, 88

H

Hawthorns, The 17, 55
H.M.P. Gartree housing 55–56, 80

117

H.M. Queen Elizabeth II 77
   – Coronation 98–99
   – Jubilee celebrations 99 –100
Hollies, The 15, 49
Holmes Farm 51, 103
Hundle Lane (See Undle Lane)
Hunter Report 1865 11

I

Iron Age 3, 13

K

Kemsley, Viscount 46, 77–78

L

Laurels, The 47, 80, 103
Local Government 5, 12
Lord of the Manor (See also Paget)
   – Baud 6, 7
   – Brooke, Sir Basil 8, 59–60
   – Crewe, Sir Ranulph 8, 76
   – Wright, John 9, 46, 60
   – Wright, Samuel 9, 59, 76
Lubenham Lodge 31, 103
Lubenham Wharf 18
Lutyens, Sir Edwin 45, 75

M

Manor Farm 9, 46, 61, 103
Mill House, The 50, 103

N

Naseby, Battle of 8–9, 28, 76
Normans 4–5

O

Old Bake House, The 53, 63
Old Hall, The 6, 8, 9, 28, 41–43, 90
Old Vicarage, The 48, 75
Olympic torch ii

P

Paget Arms 11, 60, 68, 90
Paget, Guy 9, 85, 89, 99, 101
Paget, Lord Reginald 9, 76, 101
Papillon, David (1581–1658) 43, 75
Papillon, David (1691–1762) 43,
   107–109

Papillon Hall 15, 23, 41, 43, 80, 84,
   107–109
Parish administration 9–12, 14
Paupers 9–11, 60
Perkins
   – Joshua 11, 31, 47, 54, 69, 71,
   73–74
   – Thomas 67, 69, 71
Pipers Piece 53, 66
Playing fields 89
Poor Law 11
Post Office 16, 66

R

Railway station 12, 20–24, 54, 74
Red Cow, The (See The Coach &
   Horses)
Reformation, The 27–28
Ridge and furrow 57
Rimmington, Eli & Son 32, 53, 67
Road A4304 (A427) 3, 14–15,
   17, 24
Romans 3–4, 13
Rose Cottage 49, 65, 103
Rugby to Stamford Railway 20–24

S

St Mary's Transport 17, 68
Scarecrow Festival 95–96
School, All Saints C of E Primary
   (See also Education) 12, 33–40, 74
   – building 34–36
   – governance 36, 39–40
Shops 16, 62–66, 50
Stables 46, 47, 52, 53, 68
Straw, Linda 31

T

Thorpe Lubenham Hall 15, 41,
   45–46, 54, 76, 90
Tower House, The 51–52
Turnpike roads 14–15
Trades and businesses 66–68

U

Undle Lane 3, 13

Index

V

Verger's Cottage 48
Victoria Mills (See Factories)
Village Green (See Green Gardens)
Village Hall 79, 85–87

W

War Memorial 79, 97–98
Water mill 7
Water supply 12
Wernher, Capt. George 31, 79
Wernher, Sir Harold & Lady Zia 46,
    76–77, 85, 101, 104
Western Villa 54, 55, 65
White House, The 50, 60, 65
Windmill 8, 50, 63
Wolwardington family 6, 7, 47
Workhouse 9–11
World War II 23, 39, 45, 61, 79–83,
    85, 90
    – American service personnel
    80–81, 90
    – Home Guard 83
    – V.E. Day 97
    – Women's Land Army 81, 83

Y

Yeomanry 84